Des Moines and Polk County:
Flag on the Prairie

"Partners in Progress" by Denny Rehder

Produced in cooperation with
the Polk County Historical Society

Windsor Publications, Inc
Northridge, California

Des Moines and Polk County:
Flag on the Prairie
Barbara Beving Long

"Including its heart, Des Moines, the New Style American City"

Title page: "Terrace Hill", B.F. Allen's magnificient mansion afforded the vantage point for this 1876 lithographic bird's eye view of Des Moines. The entire city is seen in this look down Sycamore Avenue (Grand Avenue) from today's Governor's mansion. Courtesy, Terrace Hill Authority

Title page, inset: Photo by Dana Downie

Windsor Publications, Inc.—History Books Division
Managing Editor: Karen Story
Design Director: Alexander D'Anca

Staff for *Des Moines and Polk County: Flag on the Prairie*
Manuscript Editor: Nora Perren
Photo Editor: Cameron Cox
Text Production Editor: Doreen Nakakihara
Editor, Corporate Biographies: Judy Hunter
Production Editor, Corporate Biographies: Phyllis Gray
Senior Proofreader: Susan J. Muhler
Editorial Assistants: Didier Beauvoir, Thelma Fleischer, Kim Kievman, Rebecca Kropp, Michael Nugwynne, Kathy B. Peyser, Pat Pittman, Theresa J. Solis
Publisher's Representatives, Corporate Biographies: Tim Burke, Roxanne Landman
Layout Artist, Corporate Biographies: John T. Wolff
Layout Artist, Editorial: Robaire Ream
Designer: Bradford Boston

Library of Congress Cataloging-in-Publication Data
Long, Barbara Beving.
   Des Moines and Polk County: flag on the prairie / Barbara Beving Long.—1st ed.
   "Produced in cooperation with the Polk County Historical Society."
   Bibliography: p. 156
   Includes index.
ISBN: 0-89781-234-4
   1. Polk County (Iowa)—History. 2. Polk County (Iowa)—Description and travel—Views. 3. Polk County (Iowa)—Industries. 4. Des Moines (Iowa)—History. 5. Des Moines (Iowa)—Description—Views. 6. Des Moines (Iowa)—Industries. I. Polk County Historical Society (Iowa) II. Title.
F627.P7L66   1988   977.7'58—dc19   88-5641
CIP

©1988 Windsor Publications, Inc.
All rights reserved
Published 1988
Printed in the United States of America
First Edition

Windsor Publications, Inc.
Elliot Martin, Chairman of the Board
James L. Fish III, Chief Operating Officer
Michele Sylvestro, Vice President/Sales-Marketing

CONTENTS

A 1908 Mason automobile tackles the capitol steps with its mighty two-cylinder engine. Courtesy, State Historical Society of Iowa

Acknowledgments   9

CHAPTER ONE
West of the Red Rock Line   11

CHAPTER TWO
Newcomers and New Challenges   19

CHAPTER THREE
Flag on the Prairie   31

CHAPTER FOUR
An Enterprising Place   45

CHAPTER FIVE
Changes with the New Century   61

CHAPTER SIX
Beyond Subsistence   79

CHAPTER SEVEN
Heritage of Achievement   99

CHAPTER EIGHT
Partners in Progress   109

Bibliography   155

Index   157

To the devoted local historians—past, present,
and future—especially the Polk County Historical Society.

This photograph from around 1890 of Silas W. McClain's store in Grimes reveals the diversity of goods available even in a town only four years old. Mr. and Mrs. McClain and their daughter Mable, shown behind the counter, operated the second store to open in Grimes. In addition to his store duties, McClain was Postmaster between 1885 and 1894 and Mayor in 1906. Located on F.M. Hubbell's and Jefferson S. Polk's St. Louis, Des Moines & Northern Railroad (later the Chicago, Milwaukee & St. Paul), Grimes was a stop for the traveling salesmen representing Des Moines wholesalers. The former store still stands in Grimes, although it has been moved from Main Street and converted to a home. Courtesy, Rev. and Mrs. Harry F. Stickle

ACKNOWLEDGMENTS

Des Moines, the county seat of Polk County, began as an Indian Agency and Army post in 1843. In the succeeding 145 years Polk County shed its military origins to become the leading county in Iowa. As the county seat and, beginning in 1857, the state capital, Des Moines soon became the center for Iowa politics, population, and commerce. Polk County pioneers indeed planted their "flag on the prairie."

As the waters of the Raccoon and Des Moines rivers have flowed together for centuries in present Polk County, so the story of this place is that of a stream of inhabitants arriving over the decades. Collectively, their actions define the history of Polk County. The contribution of these home builders, merchants, and farmers is as important and as compelling as that of the founder of the county's first life insurance company or the first elected politician.

In presenting an admittedly brief account of the county's history, I have tried to point out the important themes that illustrate Polk County and Des Moines over a proud 145-year history, and to celebrate the major events—the growth of the insurance and mining industries, the Des Moines Plan of government, the first railroad—along with the not so major incidents: the songs written about Des Moines and the kinds of foods a customer could purchase in the 1840s. I have also touched upon important events not often covered in earlier county histories, such as the women's suffrage movement and the many ethnic groups represented in the county.

Not all who pick up this book will want to read it from cover to cover. But if they have even a passing interest in people and events that came before them, they will find something—a photograph, a map, or a caricature—of interest. Many will wonder why a given subject was not mentioned; it is regrettable that the work cannot be truly comprehensive.

The photographs found here often illustrate an event discussed in the text. For example, a map drawn in 1722 shows "Le Moingona R." (the Des Moines River), source of the name "Des Moines." A rare photograph of South Park mine shows the first commercial coal mine in the county. Other illustrations show rare views of life in Polk County: a Mitchelville newspaper office in the 1910s, a nineteenth century Scandinavian boarding house from the east side of Des Moines, Abram Clegg's octagon house that once stood in what is now West Des Moines, and downtown Ankeny in the 1940s.

The photograph collection of the State Historical Society of Iowa provided a significant number of photographs reproduced here. But the Pioneer Club of Des Moines and the late Paul Ashby made this work unique. The club graciously opened its important collection of photographs—many of them never before published—for this project. Paul Ashby spent decades studying and deciphering these photographs, and the notes he left behind were invaluable. His strong interest in local history has been important to many, including me, and he will be missed. In sponsoring this project, the Polk County Historical Society has demonstrated its commitment to preserving and enjoying local history.

In closing, I can but reiterate the plea historian Nettie Sanford prefaced her Polk County history with in 1874:

The writer of this work claims but little literary ambition; and when the critics of Des Moines and Polk County read these pages, we ask a charitable judgement. We only intend to "blaze the way" for an abler pen, in chronicling the history of Polk County pioneers.

The first annual Mesquakie Indian Powwow was held in 1927 in Altoona. The celebration, which now takes place in Tama County, occurs at the end of the summer growing season when the "leaf-falling" moon nears. Games, tribal dances, and socializing are among the activities, and together they afford residents a rare glimpse of an ancient way of life. Courtesy, State Historical Society of Iowa

CHAPTER ONE

West of the Red Rock Line

Polk County as it exists today is a set of arbitrary boundaries imposed upon the rich prairie landscape. Centuries before its political establishment in 1846, glacial and geological forces shaped it, and in the process created some of the most fertile farmland in the world. The appearance of most of Polk County's 594 square miles stems from glacial action, ending with the Wisconsin glacier thousands of years ago. An east-west line crossing the county at Rising Sun, Des Moines, and West Des Moines separates the land marked by the glacier from the land it left untouched. The boundary line occurs at the foot of the capitol grounds and also at Terrace Hill, the governor's mansion.

To the north of this line of glacial demarcation the steady advance and retreat of ice sheets scoured the land, depositing rubble and filling existing water courses 14,000 years ago. The result was an expanse of broad and open space, a "prairie plain." In addition to waves of grasses, goldenrod, and prairie phlox, bogs, waterways, and groves also dotted the rolling landscape. At the end of the glacial period, the Des Moines, Raccoon, and Skunk rivers recarved their valleys in Polk County, reimposing sinuous routes upon the newly scraped and filled landscape.

A series of Native American peoples visited central Iowa, staying along or near these main rivers. The Paleo-Indian culture was present between 8,500 and 10,000 years ago, followed by the Archaic culture from 4,000 to 8,000 years ago. Between at least A.D. 650 and 1200, people of the Woodland culture dominated central Iowa. The low burial mounds they constructed for their dead were a distinguishing cultural feature. Often placed in clusters, the mounds contained the remains of the deceased (sometimes cremated), burial offerings, and objects used in daily life. According to early chroniclers of Polk County history, there were 15 such burial mounds on a terrace above the confluence of the Des Moines and Raccoon rivers. One was located a few feet south of the present courthouse, but no evi-

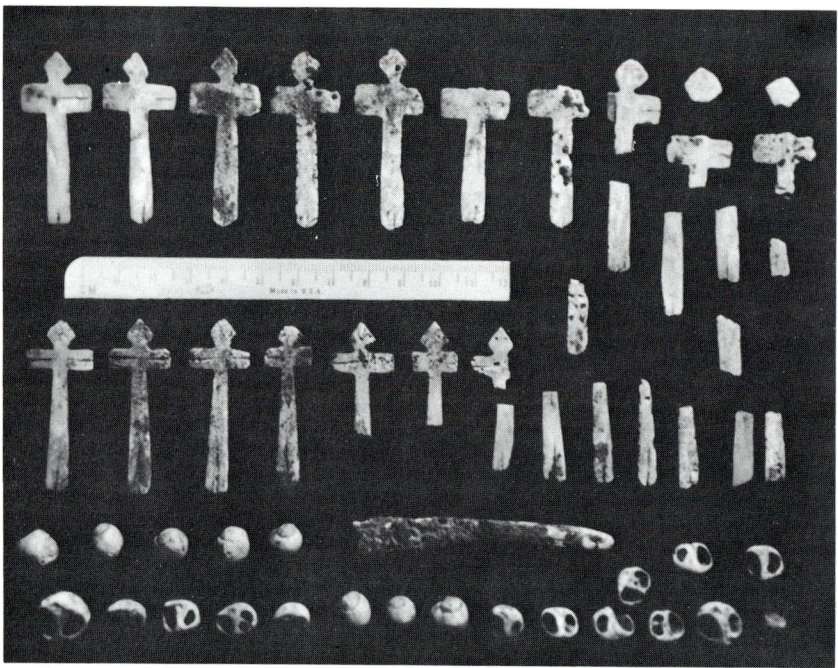

When these Great Oasis artifacts were unearthed in West Des Moines, thousands of curious residents visited the site over one July weekend in 1963. Great Oasis traders used the crosses and beads made of shell several hundred years before the Christian era. Members of the Great Oasis culture are known to have lived in South Dakota, central Iowa, southwest Minnesota, and part of Nebraska. Courtesy, State Historical Society of Iowa

dence of these mounds remains today.

Woodland burial mounds frequently occurred near camps and villages, at sites such as the mouth of the Raccoon River. Later cultures, like the Oneota (ancestors of the Ioway and Oto Indians) and the Great Oasis Complex, also lived close to the riverfronts. There was some overlap in the time these peoples spent in the Des Moines Valley— roughly between A.D. 750 and the 1300s. However, the Oneota may have lived in central Iowa as late as the 1600s.

The cultures which came after the Woodland Indians eschewed burial mounds but did establish cemeteries. In 1963 construction workers in West Des Moines uncovered a large burial place from the Great Oasis period (from perhaps A.D. 900 to 1300). Although most of the site was bulldozed before proper salvage efforts could occur, the remains of at least 18 people, as well as snail-shell beads and unusual shells cut in a cross pattern, were recovered. Probably used for trading, the cross-shaped shells were stylized representations of natural phenomena, not evidence of contact with Christian cultures.

By the 1700s, the Ioways had succeeded the Oneota and Great Oasis cultures as hunters and traders in Iowa. Also, the Sauk and Mesquakie extended their territory from the Mississippi River west into the Des Moines Valley. Challenged and threatened by French fur traders, the Sauk and Mesquakie moved from their lands along Lake Superior and near present-day Green Bay, Wisconsin, to sites on both sides of the Mississippi River. They were the last Indian culture to own the lands that constitute central Iowa.

Beginning with the explorations of Louis Jolliet and Father Jacques Marquette in 1673, areas including present-day Iowa were no longer the exclusive domain of the Native American. These explorers, the first white men to view the Des Moines River, ventured some six miles from its mouth at the Mississippi River into the interior. They saw two Indian villages along the river; one was Moinguena (spelling varies).

Because of the early Indian presence at the Raccoon River fork of the Des Moines River, it is appropriate that the present name of Des Moines preserves, albeit in a modified manner, a Native American tribal name. With the tendency to shorten unfamiliar words, the waterway

on which the village of the Moinguena occurred was shown on maps as "la riviere des Moingona" (the river of the Moingonas) in 1703, the "R. de Moines" in 1804, and the "River de Moine" in 1824. The name "Des Moines" is a Frenchified Indian name which recalls the early Native American and French presence in Iowa.

Conflict with other tribes, persistent encroachment on former Indian territory by white men, successive land treaties that diminished Indian-held lands, and the need for spots well-stocked with game combined to push the Sauk and Mesquakie westward from the Mississippi River. Contact between Indian tribes and representatives of the U.S. government increased during the early 1800s. Successive secretaries of war established forts and appointed Indian agents to mediate problems among the various tribes now competing for the same space in the Mississippi River Valley. Indian agents also enforced treaties between the United States and various tribes and saw to the payment of tribal annuities.

Indian agents and the traders they licensed provided the main contact between whites and Indians west of the Mississippi. As early as 1824 trader Maurice Blondeau opened a temporary trading post at Dirt Lodge, located at the Raccoon River fork of the "River de Moine." Indian agent Thomas Forsyth lim-

This mural in the Polk County Courthouse by the nationally known New York artist Douglas Volk depicts contact between fur traders, missionaries, and Indians in Iowa. Traders bargained with the Sioux, Sauk and Mesquakie, and Ioway for the season's catch in the Des Moines River Valley as early as 1799. Courtesy, State Historical Society of Iowa

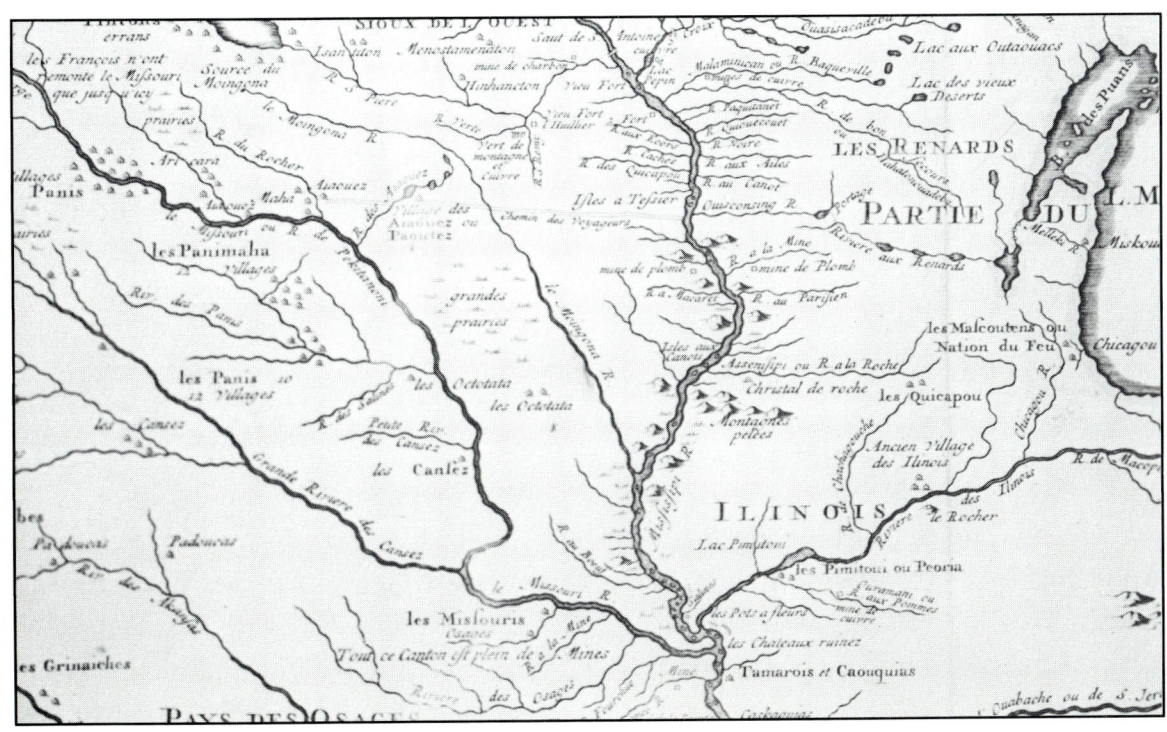

This 1722 map, though less than accurate, clearly shows the distinctive outline of the Mississippi River where it forms the eastern boundary of Iowa. "Le Moingona" is an early name for the Des Moines River and shows how the name was derived from the Moingona Indian village. Courtesy, State Historical Society of Iowa

This portrait of Keokuk dates from a visit he made to Washington, D.C., and other eastern cities in 1837. An accomplished orator, Keokuk charmed the dignitaries, noting that the Great Spirit "made the same sky above our heads for both" peoples. Keokuk was an astute leader who achieved good relations with U.S. government officials. Courtesy, Des Moines Pioneer Club

ited the license to run from autumn to spring, when the Sauk and Mesquakie hunted in the interior. Dirt Lodge was only a temporary outpost, but it represented a step in white advancement into the Indian lands that would become Polk County.

In the nineteenth century Sauk and Mesquakie chiefs became all too familiar with treaties with the white man. The Sauk and Mesquakie, singly or together, ceded land through no less than 11 treaties with the government between 1789 and 1842. In the treaty of 1842, the Sauk and Mesquakie agreed to leave their villages along the lower Des Moines, Skunk, and Iowa rivers by May 1, 1843, move west of the Red Rock Line to the Raccoon River fork, and remain there until October 11, 1845.

The Red Rock Line was named for the red-hued rocks in present Marion County on the Des Moines River where the line bisected the state. It divided the area open for legal white settlement to the east from the Indian-held lands to the west. Under provisions of the treaty, the Sauk and Mesquakie were to receive a $40,000 annuity and move to the Kansas Territory following their brief final stay in present Polk County.

Located at the fork of the Des Moines and Raccoon rivers, the second Fort Des Moines (the first, located on the Mississippi River near present-day Montrose in Lee County, existed from 1834 to 1837) and the Indian Agency

were established as temporary outposts, in use only until white settlement commenced in 1845. The Indian agent oversaw Indian activities. Under Captain James Allen, the military patrolled the region to prohibit illegal white settlement and to protect the resident Sauk and Mesquakie from rival tribes. Allen also prepared for the eventual transfer of ownership to United States citizens. During the joint military and Indian occupation at the Raccoon River fork, an estimated 200 whites connected with the fort and the agency and 2,300 Sauk and Mesquakie lived in the vicinity.

In 1843 Indian agent Major John Beach established operations on the east side of the Des Moines River, about a half mile from the future capitol site. In addition to the log agency house, a smokehouse, stables, and blacksmith shop were built on a site overlooking the Des Moines River plain and the Indian villages below.

The Sauk and Mesquakie built bark-covered lodges in four villages under the leadership of Keokuk, Poweshiek, Wishecomaque, and Powsheshemone. Major Beach reported in September 1843 that about half the Sauk and one band of Mesquakie had their villages within sight of the agency. The rest of the Sauk lived within eight miles of it, but most of the Mesquakie, led by Poweshiek, preferred a site some 15 miles away on the Skunk River.

In May of 1843 Captain James Allen led his dragoons to the Raccoon River fork. Five civilian carpenters and two brickmakers helped build Fort Des Moines No. 2. Enlisted men's quarters lay in a string along the Raccoon River. The officers' quarters were built in a row along the Des Moines River, making a V-shaped encampment. Recent archaeological excavations have turned up part of a hearth from one of these 1843 officers' cabins.

When they left for Kansas in 1845, the Mesquakie longed for the familiar well-stocked hunting grounds of Iowa. In 1856 they persuaded the Iowa General Assembly to allow them to return and buy land. The initial 80 acre purchase was the beginning of the Mesquakie Settlement which now covers 3,300 acres in Tama County. This early twentieth century photograph of the Mesquakie Settlement shows typical reed-covered wickiups. Courtesy, State Historical Society of Iowa

Nearly 40 percent of Iowa land was distributed to holders of federal land warrants who were military veterans seeking farmland or speculators who had purchased the veteran's warrants. For his military service, Jeremiah Cory received this land warrant for 160 acres. Courtesy, Des Moines Pioneer Club

Associated with the fort and agency were blacksmiths to care for the Indians' horses, a tailor, doctors, gunsmiths, farmers to provide fodder and produce, and fur traders. Not all were paragons of virtue. One trader, Alexander Turner, received a contract to supply produce, but lost it after illegally selling liquor to the Indians. Trader Josiah Smart served as an interpreter; he brought two black women with him to Iowa and later sold them as slaves in Missouri.

The land west of the Red Rock Line stood poised to host the onslaught of land-hungry pioneers. At the stroke of midnight on a moonlit October night in 1845, Beach ordered a gun fired to announce the beginning of legal settlement. Eager settlers fired answering volleys and rushed to stake claims. Jeremiah Church "set fire to some of the old Indian houses for a light to mark out his new possessions," according to Nettie Sanford, a historian from the period. Another historian, H.B. Turrill, painted a memorable picture of men laying out claims:

Ere long the landscape was shrouded in darkness, save the wild and fitful glaring of torches, carried by the claim-makers. Before the night had entirely worn away, the rough surveys were finished, and the Indian lands had found new tenants. Throughout the country thousands of acres were laid off in claims before dawn.

At the former fort, newcomers appropriated the soldiers' quarters, converting them to dwellings, a school, stores, a newspaper office, the first courtroom, and a tavern. Calvin Thornton, an 1840s arrival, recalled stepping out from his shop and shooting rabbits in the dense hazelnut brush that blanketed the site of Des Moines. Upon coming to the place in 1855, longtime resident Tacitus Hussey found it "a dirty, smokey little place."

In the countryside, settlers chose sites near good water and timber

This image, a detail from a 1914 mural painted by Des Moines artist Charles Atherton Cumming for the Polk County Courthouse, depicts the departure of the Indians from west of the Red Rock Line. The military patrolled against illegal white settlement until the night of October 11, 1845, when Major John Beach ordered a gun fired to announce legal settlement. Courtesy, State Historical Society of Iowa

sources. Early settlements developed near Four Mile Creek and its east branch, the Swan and Byers branches of the Skunk River, and Big Creek in the late 1840s. Settlers T.K. Brooks and the John S. Dean family took over earlier claims of the fur traders in Lee Township, now the east side of Des Moines.

Many of the early settlers opted for the east and southeast parts of the county, but settler George Beebe chose a waterside site in the distant northwest sector, near the Des Moines River. After spending a night in May 1846 at the Pennsylvania House in Fort Des Moines—where a meal could be had for 10 cents, 15 if you had biscuits made from white flour—he moved on to Madison Township and homesteaded on a hill with a view of the river. In 1847 he helped lay a road past his place; three years later he platted Polk City on the site of Waconsa, an old Indian camp.

These and other settlers arrived after legal settlement was allowed but in advance of such useful elements as land surveys (undertaken in 1847), roads, or even a county seat. Undeterred, county residents numbered 1,792 strong in 1847 and 4,214 two years later, a 135 percent increase. The stage was set for dramatic changes on the landscape. In an 1848 guidebook, George B. Sargent, later mayor of Davenport, noted that Iowa "has commenced its career with prospects of far more than ordinary brilliancy."

Located at the bottom of a hill, the tracks of the Wabash Railroad marked the south boundary of Runnells beginning in the 1880s. James O. Lamb, pictured here around 1910, operated a draying service in town and is shown loading his wagon with goods to haul up the hill to Main Street merchants. Courtesy, Delmar Schell

CHAPTER TWO

Newcomers and New Challenges

In the 1840s, travelers through the Iowa Territory wrote about their journeys, expressing preconceived notions that are little changed today. A description penned in 1848 pointed out:

An idea prevails at the East, that the prairies are uniformly level. This is by no means the case. Sometimes, indeed, they are spread out in boundless plains: but the high, or upland prairies, which are much the most beautiful, as well as the best adapted to cultivation, present a series of graceful undulations not unlike the swell of the sea, from which they derive the appellation "rolling."

Early guidebooks for lands in the West emphasized the positive aspects in their commentaries, and it seemed that every new county was a repository for all the most desirable resources, scenery, and prospects. Polk County was described as filled with "rolling prairie, with a due proportion of timber," and "well-watered with rivers and creeks, the banks of which abound in coal, lime, sandstone, and gypsum in great quantities."

In 1846, when the county was in its first year, John B. Newhall, author of *A Glimpse of Iowa in 1846*, declared he knew of "no interior point presenting more flattering prospects." He noted the advantages that "nature has so lavishly bestowed": the navigable Des Moines River, the waterpower suitable for mills, and the prairie that was "remarkably fertile and productive."

The guidebooks—dreambooks really—enticed the Eastern farmer, weary of eking out a living from exhausted soil. The glowing descriptions of the Iowa prairies fired their imaginations as they surveyed their meager resources and made the difficult decision to move to an unknown and largely uninhabited place. Of the 9,417 people in Polk County in 1856, 8,529 were born in America. Sons and daughters from the older states populated both Polk County and the Hawkeye State.

Indiana and Ohio were the best represented in 1856, together contributing 3,933 people to the county. Internal migration within the state accounted for

Surrounded by wild fruit trees, the Mitchell family's way station, Apple Grove, was the only refuge between Tool's Point (now Monroe) and Fort Des Moines in 1844. The Mitchells sold the cabin in 1846 and built a larger stagecoach stop a few miles away. The Green Wheeler family, pictured here in this rare image from 1887, bought the farmstead in 1851. Note the small cage housing the pet songbird at the entrance. The man with the gun, Henry Wheeler, is calling to his hunting dogs, wishing to include them in the picture. Courtesy, Merle E. Reed

1,573 Iowa-born residents in Polk County, making Iowa the third-ranking place of birth. In all, 27 states and the District of Columbia were represented in the county in 1856. Germany, Ireland, and England contributed 577 of the 888 foreign-born.

Pioneer life of the 1840s and 1850s was hardly the idyllic word picture painted by the guidebooks. Local historian Nettie Sanford wrote about L.M. Burk, who in 1846 built a 16-by-12-foot log cabin west of Mud Creek for his family of 14. By day all the bedding was piled upon one bed, with "trunks, baskets, bags and bundles" beneath. "On the walls were hung old hats, cloaks, shawls and great coats, in fact the cabin was lined with wearing apparel and household utensils . . ." At night the beds were placed on the floor, and the table put outside "to hold the moonshine."

Living in a rude log cabin on an isolated homestead brought the farm family close to the elements. In scorching summer heat men donned protective mittens and coats, "vails [sic] even," against marauding mosquitoes up near George Beebe's cabin on the upper Des Moines River. And imagine spending the winter in a drafty cabin heated by a smoky fire and scented with the odor of unwashed bodies. In Bloomfield Township, the H.C. Hargis family spent the winter of 1853-1854 in a dwelling with four rooms—if quilts for partitions can really make four rooms.

Half of those listing occupations in the 1856 census came to Polk County

NEWCOMERS AND NEW CHALLENGES

The simple way of life on this farmstead is evident. An ax, a two-man crosscut saw, and a bow saw were used to provide firewood. The old wood washstand included a rocking device used to swish the clothing in the wash water. Both the metal washtub and milkcan date the picture as from the late nineteenth century. The old wood washstand, however, could be as old as the 1850s log cabin. Courtesy, Des Moines Pioneer Club

to farm, although only 256 actually had title to the productive lands upon which they toiled. The prairie soil ran from 3 to 15 feet and the topsoil layer averaged 12 to 14 inches of fecundity. By 1856, 33,108 of the total 201,978 acres of land had been improved, the dense mat of prairie sod turned.

The pioneer farmer grew spring and winter wheat, oats, corn, and potatoes, raised hogs and cattle, and sold butter, cheese, and wool. It was a diverse agricultural economy, not based on a single commodity. A few harvested such exotica as hops, maple sugar, rye, or apples. Bloomfield Township farmers, many of whom hailed from Kentucky, planted apple orchards on the hilly countryside overlooking the Des Moines River valley; in fact, the township was named for the blooming hillsides of fruit.

Bloomfield Township farmers supplied produce to a growing population in Des Moines. While living conditions were primitive by modern standards, residents did enjoy a variety of goods and services. In an 1849 advertisement in the *Iowa Star*, Des Moines' first newspaper, merchant James Campbell boasted that such delicacies as peach brandy and Madeira wines, as well as staples such as sugar and coffee, and dry goods of "cassimeres, alpaca, satinets, and tweeds" were kept "constantly on hand" in his store, the former guardhouse of Fort Des Moines No. 2.

The early settlement period for Polk County coincided with the era of steamboat travel, especially on the Mississippi. Indeed, one of the justifications for creation of a fort at the Raccoon River fork was the suitability of the Des Moines River as a navigable waterway, at least for the shallower variety of steamboats. Steamboats regularly plied the Missouri River from St. Louis all the way to Montana during this period, so the plans for river travel to Des Moines were not unreasonable.

Steamboats with such euphonious titles as the *Flora Temple, De Moine Belle, Pandodging,* and *Movestar* docked in Des

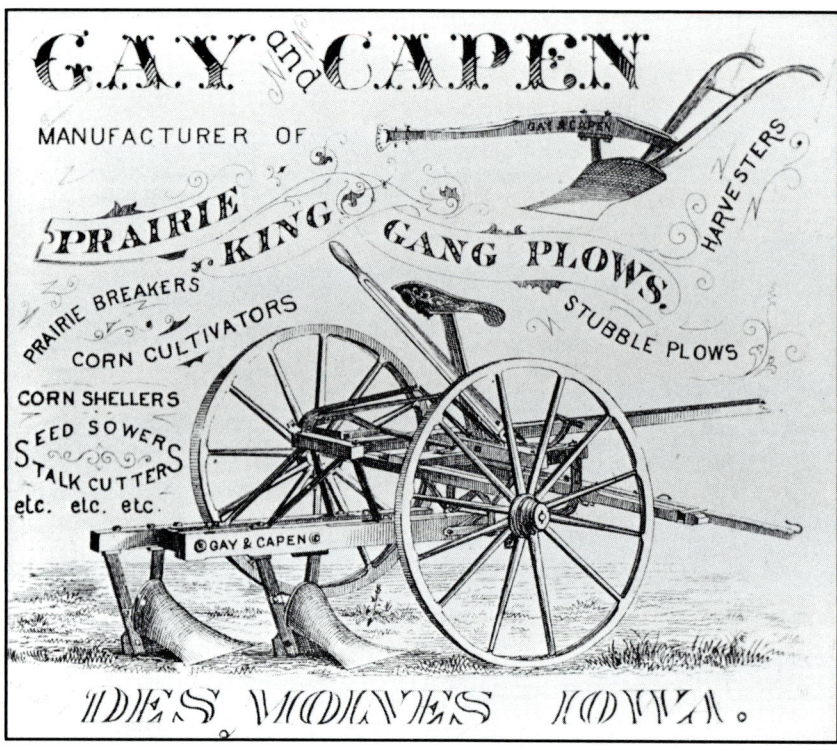

Gay & Capen provided a full range of agricultural implements in the 1870s for the Polk County farmer. Equipment for breaking the prairie sod, sowing seed, cultivating between rows of corn, or harvesting crops could be purchased through them. From Andreas' Atlas of Iowa, *1875*

Moines. Steamboats anchored in Des Moines at least 41 times during the high water periods of the 1850s, the peak time for river travel to Polk County, but the curves and bends and shallow sections of the river made navigation a difficult and seasonal event.

Steamboats provided one means for access to Polk County, a network of roads another. With the expectation of increased white settlement in the late 1840s, government officials authorized the construction of roads into the hinterlands. Military, territorial, and soon state and county roads allowed pioneers to reach the New Purchase, as the lands west of the Red Rock Line were then called, and settlement occurred along these routes.

When the river fork was still a garrison under military control, Captain Allen began a road survey between it and Tool's Point (now Monroe in Jasper County) to connect with the road to Keokuk. Four Mile Road, the first substantial overland route to Des Moines, connected early settlements in the county such as Apple Grove and Rising Sun and crossed Peter Newcomer's bridge over Four Mile Creek before reaching Fort Des Moines.

The second major road connected the county with Iowa City in 1845, when it was still the territorial capital. The route entered Beaver Township, where it crossed the dreaded Skunk River. Travel involving the Skunk River—even if it only happened once—left a strong and negative impression. Writing 55 years after crossing, one writer described it as "a stream the most sinuous in the world, which seemingly required only a spattering of rain to convert it into a roaring torrent or a miniature sea," depending on the riverbank height. En route to the Colorado mines near Pike's Peak in 1859, Romanzo Kingman recalled using double teams to pull wagons for over a mile in the axle-deep mud of the "long dreaded Skunk bottoms."

Regular stagecoach service to Des Moines began in 1849 with establishment of the first trans-state route between Keokuk and Council Bluffs. Thus Des Moines was on a vital transportation route only three years after the last soldiers vacated the fort. The last coach came through Des Moines in 1870, a casualty of railroad supremacy.

Iowa lay in the path of California-bound gold miners, Mormons, and other emigrants seeking new lands in the West. In one of the greatest settlement pushes ever, nearly 300,000 people were on the move between 1840 and 1860 in the plains states, with an estimated 50,000 heading west in 1850 alone. A major bottleneck in Polk County occurred along the Des Moines River as impatient travelers lined up on the dirt roads awaiting ferry service at Des Moines, Dudley, Adelphi, and Freel. Until the first bridge was built in 1855, ferries offered the only means to cross besides wading. During six wet weeks in the spring of 1850, 1,049 teams carrying 2,813 people crossed the Des Moines River in the county. Newspaper accounts from the time described continuous lines of westward-moving wagons as far as the eye could see.

Des Moines became the state capital in 1857, an event which launched a spate of state-authorized road-building across the state. Remote communities scrambled to acquire transportation connections to the new capital in the interior. The legislature authorized an unprecedented 19 new state roads radiating in all directions. All led to Polk County or intersected with a road that did. When combined with the eight other roads to Polk County dating from 1843 to 1855, the prospects for the new capital and its hinterland were considerable.

The new roads encouraged settlement along them. Avon was platted in 1856 on the road to Knoxville. Located

In 1866 local photographer J.P. Sharmon took this remarkably clear photograph of the Walnut Street bridge in Des Moines shortly after it opened in the fall. Colonel S.F. Spofford headed the committee who contracted with the Clinton Bridge Company to build the Howe wood truss bridge. Spofford's interest was understandable, for he operated the Demoine House shown at the west end of the bridge. Now travelers could easily cross the toll bridge over the Des Moines River to stay at his hostelry or buy "liquor, cigars and tobacco" across the street. Courtesy, State Historical Society of Iowa

"Colonel" Edward F. Hooker, probably seated next to the driver, ably assumed the reins of the Western Stage Company in Des Moines in 1855. As superintendent, he was responsible for the high quality of service the company offered. During the Civil War, Hooker provided free rides to veterans wounded in battle. By 1866, the company offered daily connections to the railroad, which had reached Kellogg 22 miles from Des Moines. Courtesy, Des Moines Pioneer Club

in Polk's southeast tip, it was a thriving community in the 1860s, with stores, a hotel, 20 houses, and a Brethren church.

As important as the spokes of roads were to developing Polk County, the arrival of the railroad had even more significance. The profound effects of railroad service upon a place would be difficult to overstate. Railroads supplanted steamboats, stagecoaches, plank roads, canals, river locks, and dams as the latest in transportation technology. They brought a more efficient means of moving commodities, goods, and people. Their construction ended rural isolation and opened areas for settlement previously accessible only by uncertain, difficult roads.

The advent of this new technology created an avalanche of land speculation, new town building, and general economic expansion wherever the rails were laid.

Polk County residents worked for 15 years to get the railroad. Construction of the Des Moines Valley Railroad (originally known as the Keokuk, Fort Des Moines & Minnesota Railroad) extended between Keokuk and Ottumwa in 1859. Delay set in with the Civil War, and in the early 1860s the company reorganized and construction plans resumed. Competition from other counties seeking the rail route prompted Polk County residents to raise $100,000 for the railroad company.

On August 29, 1866, the great day finally arrived. Des Moines residents turned out in force to celebrate the inaugural train. "Gaily decorated with flags and mottoes," it carried 300 riders and dignitaries on the seven and a half hour trip from Keokuk. The celebration occurred on the east side of town since there was no railroad bridge until 1869 for the Des Moines Valley line. The whole town seemed to have turned out to witness the momentous occasion, and local historian Tacitus Hussey recalled "a wilderness of handkerchiefs, hats and hands waving from the windows of the cars."

Arriving in 1867, the Chicago, Rock Island & Pacific Railroad was the second

Thomas Mitchell and his family operated the first inn in Polk County. In the 1850s they charged 12.5 cents for a meal of side pork, cornbread, and milk and pledged to "dispense comfort to the weary" and to "cheer the gloomy," according to an 1852 advertisement. In 1849 the Mitchells reportedly fed 7,000 teams belonging to pioneers bound for the West. From Andreas' Atlas of Polk County, *1875*

Polk County residents adjusted quickly to the railroad beginning in 1866. Legislators hopped the train to return home, farmers shipped pork and corn, and merchants received all manner of freight, from lumber to millinery. The first freight shipment to Des Moines was a load of lumber for the Getchell Lumber Company. It arrived August 30, 1866, the day after the great celebration for the Des Moines Valley Railroad. Courtesy, State Historical Society of Iowa

line to reach Polk County. Chicago investors organized the Rock Island, as they did many of the successful and long-standing rail lines in America. It had a more significant economic impact on the county than that of the Des Moines Valley, for it provided jobs in its repair shops as well as cross-country service.

In 1892 the Rock Island moved its repair shops to Valley Junction, a small shipping point established in 1871. There the recently acquired Sibley, Winterset and Indianola branch of the Rock Island and also the Minneapolis & St. Louis Railroad crossed the main east-west Rock Island line. Although Des Moines residents continued to use passenger and freight depots in the Capital City, Valley Junction became the terminal division station with repair and machine shops and administrative offices for the Rock Island line in Iowa.

To take advantage of the new development at Valley Junction, two pioneer Des Moines families, the Casadys and the Youngermans, formed Hawkeye Investment Company in 1890. They platted the town of Valley Junction two years later and offered building lots and housing for the hundreds of railroad employees transferred there. Growth was immediate and dramatic; in 1905 Valley Junction had 1,411 residents, and 3,026 10 years later.

The Des Moines Valley Railroad and the Rock Island line were only the begin-

The wreck of the Rock Island train at Four Mile Creek was the worst ever in central Iowa. On a stormy night in August 1877, flood waters swept away the stone underpinnings of the railroad bridge. The engineer could not see that only part of the bridge stood. He opened the throttle, and the train hurtled into the water. Twenty died and 35 were injured. Courtesy, Des Moines Pioneer Club

ning. By the 1880s five major lines crossed Iowa from east to west, and numerous connecting spurs created a north-south network. With its central location Iowa enjoyed transcontinental connections that amounted to 5,235 miles of track. No Iowan lived more than 25 miles from a station.

The number of new towns and stations—at least 15 in Polk County—reflected the unprecedented rate of railroad construction in Iowa throughout the last quarter of the nineteenth century. Some towns, such as Ashawa, Campbell, Nobleton, and Loring, existed only a few years. Others, including Santiago, Commerce, Farrar, and Crocker, persisted only as collections of a few houses and maybe a church. But communities such as Altoona, Ankeny, Bondurant, and Grimes achieved notable and enduring success following their beginnings as railroad stops.

The circumstances behind the birth of Ankeny, now a major suburb north of Des Moines, were typical of railroad-related town building. John F. Ankeny, a Des Moines speculator with medical training, was among the major stockholders of the Des Moines & Minneapolis Railroad. As an investor in this line to Ames, Ankeny was aware of the proposed route and bought land along it. In 1875 he platted a town into 11 blocks containing 71 lots, and named it after himself. To stimulate settlement,

Ankeny built the first hotel and general store in town. He never lived there.

There were profits in railroading for those with courage and capital. F.M. Hubbell, Jefferson Polk, and other Des Moines investors incorporated the Union Land Company to develop depot sites that became instant new towns on the prairie in the 1880s. The town-making activities dovetailed nicely with the railroad companies they organized. These shrewd capitalists later sold the short lines to transcontinental railroad companies, including the Chicago & Northwestern; Chicago, Milwaukee & St. Paul; and the Wabash Railroad. The rail stops of Runnells, Grimes, Clive, and Sheldahl all owed their genesis to business investments by these Des Moines leaders.

The founding of Bondurant in 1883 represented another variant in the creation of new rail towns—the wealthy farmer acting as town maker. Alexander C. Bondurant settled in Polk County in 1857. By the time of his death in 1899 he had increased his original 320-acre holdings to 3,000 acres. The farmer used his land to good advantage by giving the Chicago Great Western Railroad a right-of-way. To aid in town development, Bondurant donated a church site and offered free lots to anyone building commercial structures in his new town. Today the complex of lofty grain elevators—Iowa's rural skyscrapers—reflects Bondurant's continuing role as a farm shipping center.

Another category of town-making encompassed the establishment of Berwick, Mitchellville, Avon Station, Elkhart, and Grimes. All grew from existing communities that failed to gain direct railroad connections. Enterprising residents thereupon picked up their town

Valley Junction's standing as a railroad town dated from 1892, but earlier settlers also left their imprint on the landscape. The Abram Clegg house, which once stood at 6th and Ashworth Road, was probably built in 1865 and illustrates the ideas of Orson Fowler. In his 1853 book The Octagon House: A Home for All, *Fowler argued that the octagon shape was a better, more economical design. Courtesy, Des Moines Pioneer Club*

and moved it to the railroad. Grimes residents even crossed the county line to reach the Union Land Company's new town, deserting Dallas County's Osprey in the process. Thomas Mitchell, the first settler in eastern Polk County, moved not once, but twice, in hopes of gaining railroad connections, proof of the powerful pull the railroad exercised on county residents.

If a Polk County town did not get direct railroad connections, it failed to thrive. Pre-railroad settlements in the county—Rising Sun, Ivy, Polk City, and Saylorville—lacked the railroad and as a consequence failed to grow and prosper as rail towns did. Even though Polk City and Saylorville gained stations near them, no puffing, clanking locomotives spewed sooty smoke and trails of sparks into their towns, and they suffered economically as a result.

Beginning in 1866 and lasting into the 1890s, the coming of the railroads changed the countryside and stimulated the county's economy. Residents of towns and counties along a proposed route competed fiercely to gain the lifeline to lucrative markets in the East, and the chance to grow and prosper.

Nine rail lines entered Des Moines by 1881. By 1885 14 railroads and their spurs twined across the city. Rail construction and creation of new railroad companies peaked in the 1880s, and companies consolidated in the early years of the twentieth century. The hustle and bustle associated with the daily arrival of 38 passenger trains, commonplace by the 1880s, was far different from the excitement surrounding the coming of the first train to Des Moines in 1866. The whole town had set aside the day to witness the event and to celebrate.

In the field of government and politics, residents applied the same enthusiasm and skill they employed in their quest for rail service to win the county seat and the even more significant designation of capital of Iowa.

It is difficult to imagine that Clive, now a highly urbanized part of metropolitan Des Moines, was once a rural shipping point on the Milwaukee Railroad. Around the turn of the century, trains rumbled past the depot at 86th and University every half hour. Work crews, or "bridge gangs," often camped by the depot. They stayed for a week or two as they went about repairing the tracks. Frank Charles, the only one wearing a hat, was in charge of this bridge gang.

On August 8, 1885, the nation mourned the death of President U.S. Grant. To honor and pay respect to the man who led the nation through some of its most critical years, Des Moines residents gathered to attend observances at the nearly completed capitol. Courtesy, State Historical Society of Iowa

CHAPTER THREE

Flag on the Prairie

Polk County was established in 1846, when James K. Polk was the nation's 11th president. The Iowa legislature passed separate acts that established its boundaries and created the mechanism for governing, such as the offices of county sheriff, surveyor, and recorder. Although the fledgling town of Fort Des Moines was the largest settlement in central Iowa in 1846, the county seat honor was not automatically bestowed upon it. Backers of Polk City, Brooklyn, and Dudley favored their communities and promoted their cause to the legislature.

Fort Des Moines supporters employed some clever political maneuvers to secure the county seat. The goal was to gain a more central location for their community, and it was easier to tinker with the county's shape than to move the town. Thus, county boundaries were temporarily shifted six miles westward and back again in 1846 in an attempt to achieve centrality. Polk County also temporarily acquired the northern tier of Warren County's townships, which included present-day Hartford and Carlisle.

The political ploys favored Fort Des Moines. Three county seat commissioners spent eight days touring the new county, and on May 25, 1846, they designated the now more central Fort Des Moines as county seat. In the quest for the county seat, Polk County's boundaries were changed four times between 1846 and 1853, when Warren County regained all of the 144-square mile purloined strip except for a small piece north of the Des Moines River.

While the battle over county boundaries ensued, separate legislation passed in January 1846 allowed establishment of county government. The first county elections and the first county court session were both held the following April. Some of the first elected officials included civilian residents formerly attached to Fort Des Moines: Thomas Mitchell (sheriff), G.B. Clark (assessor), and John Saylor (probate judge). Others associated with the fort served on the first grand jury, including Peter Newcomer,

Civil engineer J.B. Millar surveyed and drew the plat map of what was then called Fort Des Moines in January 1854. The Original Plat included a courthouse square fronting on Court Avenue and a market place on Market Street. Horse Shoe Lake has long been filled in, and the Mississippi & Missouri Railroad Depot was never built at the then remote site near 12th and Walnut Streets. Courtesy, State Historical Society of Iowa

J.D. Parmalee, John B. Scott, and Joseph Thrift. Convening in a former garrison log cabin, the first court had little business before it. No grand jury was needed and there were no indictments or other legal business—except for fees for the 22 jurors.

The imposition of governmental organization also arrived in rural Polk County in the form of land surveys. In 1847 U.S. government surveyors finished measuring and describing the county. The U.S. Land Ordinance of 1785 imposed across the nation a geometric grid system of townships six miles square and containing 36 sections. Township and section lines separated farms and land holdings into manageable units, a necessity for orderly sales. Settlers who had arrived in advance of the surveys and had selected farmsites could now obtain legal title.

A.D. Jones, the first Polk County surveyor, started laying out the Town of Fort Des Moines in June 1846, as soon as the last soldiers left the former garrison. The next month the first sale of lots in Fort Des Moines was held. The original plat lay exclusively on the west side of the river and emanated from the garrison site at the river forks. A five-by-seven-block space contained 324 lots, a courthouse square, and a marketplace. Not to be outdone, east side residents platted the Town of Demoin, so spelled to reflect the proper pronunciation.

The rival communities might have remained separate entities but for their joint interest in being the state capital.

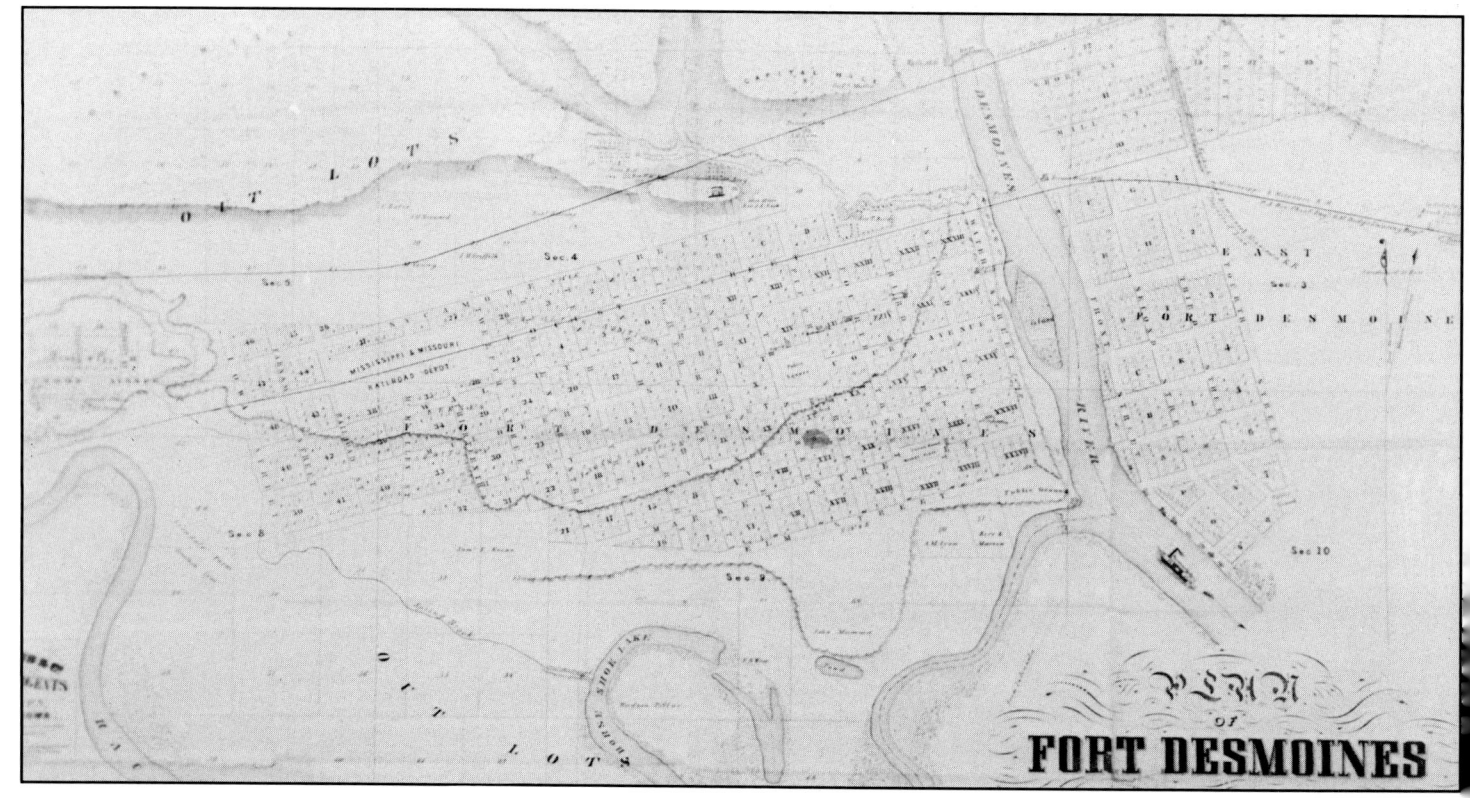

After Governor James W. Grimes decreed that the new capital was to be built "within two miles of the junction of the Des Moines and Raccoon Rivers" in Polk County, both sides temporarily set aside their differences in 1857 to make one city out of the two towns. Residents on both sides of the river therefore petitioned the legislature to incorporate the City of Des Moines, believing that the capital of Iowa should be an incorporated city, not just a town.

Interest in a more centrally located capital than Iowa City had surfaced as early as 1846, when Iowa achieved statehood. Congressman Augustus C. Dodge noted the desirability of moving the capital to a site on the Des Moines River. Other commentators were not convinced that such a move would occur. George B. Sargent noted in his 1848 guidebook to Iowa that "No one appears to entertain a serious idea that the seat of government will be removed from it [Iowa City], at least, for the next fifty years."

Des Moines residents were only one of the groups clamoring to be the capital. Supporters from Oskaloosa, Pella, Red Rock, and Tool's Point (now Monroe) all submitted petitions to the legislature favoring their locales. In the 1850-1851 legislative session, 1,662 people signed House petitions for Oskaloosa; Fort Des Moines mustered a mere 155 signatures. But in 1852-1853, 1,642 men signed Senate petitions for

At the time of this drawing, 1857, Polk County residents were enjoying the benefits that came with having Des Moines named state capital but also suffering from the nationwide economic depression. A fringe of houses, a few shops, a mill, and a woolen factory greeted arrivals on the east bank of the Des Moines River. The principle business section was on the west side, on Elm and Second streets. From Historical Reminiscences of the City of Des Moines, 1857

As the state capital, Des Moines was the obvious location for important public buildings, such as the United States Courthouse. Known as the Federal Building, or "Old Fed," its 41 rooms housed the post office, federal courts, and offices for land transactions, customs, internal revenue, and the weather bureau. Originally built in 1868 and rebuilt in 1886 to include a new tower and mansard roof, the building remained unchanged until torn down to make way for a parking ramp in 1968. Courtesy, Public Library of Des Moines

Fort Des Moines, contrasted with only 131 signatures on behalf of Oskaloosa. The delay in selecting a site helped Fort Des Moines' position, for settlement increased rapidly west of the Red Rock Line. There were 35 more counties in the newly settled areas west of Iowa City in 1854 than in 1847, and these counties all had legislative representatives. After considerable discussion and finagling lasting seven years, the General Assembly decreed in 1854 that Iowa's capital would relocate to Polk County.

Des Moines interests on both sides of the river prevailed in the fight for the capital, but differed sharply on the proper location for the capitol building. Governor Grimes appointed a five-man commission and directed them to select a site in Polk County. He also stated that both the capitol site and building were to be donated to the state. Des Moines residents competed fiercely for the privilege of giving their property to the state and paying construction costs.

Intense lobbying began for the east and west sides of the city. The west-siders offered land they said was worth $200,000 and a 20-acre tract worth $100,000 for the capitol. The east-siders offered only 17.5 acres, yet the commissioners selected the east side site.

Rumors of shenanigans—bribes of money and town lots—swept through town. Writing in his diary in 1856, Polk County deputy auditor Oscar L. Faulkner noted that "it is rumored that their (the commissioners') private purse is offered more to locate it on the east side." A state investigation prompted by angry west-siders who still hoped to have the capitol seemed to substantiate the bribery charges. Four of the five commissioners apparently received property around the east side capitol site in exchange for their vote. Those deeply involved in the site selection refused to testify, and definitive evidence was lacking. Another factor in selecting the east side site may have been that the east-siders were members of the Republican party, as was the governor, and he may have influenced the commissioners as well.

Regardless of the questions surrounding site selection, the 10-acre capitol grounds afforded a sweeping view of the Des Moines and Raccoon rivers

Polk County's second courthouse was ready for the judges, auditor, and other county officials in January 1863. Celebration of its completion was muted, for Civil War events and casualties took precedence in those dark times. Courtesy, Public Library of Des Moines

below. Governor Grimes described the "gentle swell of land" as "command[ing] a good prospect [that] seems to be well adapted to the purpose for which it has been selected." But former Lieutenant Governor B.F. Gue remembered the difficulty in reaching the spot. It was a mile from the hotels frequented by legislators, and east side streets in 1857 were "simply wagon tracks made through low, swampy river bottom, and up a steep ungraded hill" to the capitol site.

As promised, east side backers donated the capitol site and spent $35,000 on the capitol building. Although the new capitol was thrown open on July 4, 1857, for "music, dancing, good feeling, and fun," it was not ready for the opening of the 1857 legislative session.

Elected officials did move state records to Des Moines in the fall of that year. Among the items moved while Iowa had a "capitol on wheels" were four cumbersome safes. The state treasurer's safe was left stranded on the prairie while a late autumn storm raged around it. State officers were especially relieved when it arrived in Des Moines, for it contained enough gold and silver coins to pay their monthly salary.

The first capitol in Des Moines housed the seat of government for 26 years. Eventually the growing state needed a larger building. Construction of the second and present capitol in Des Moines began somewhat lamely with poor quality stone in 1871 and ended in 1886. Interior work continued into the 1900s.

The third and present Polk County courthouse was dedicated on October 31, 1906. One of Iowa's best known architectural firms, Proudfoot & Bird of Des Moines, designed the Beaux-Arts style building. A notable feature of the building's facade are the window keystones of carved grotesque faces. Courtesy, State Historical Society of Iowa

Polk County and the new capital stood on the brink of prosperity and growth in 1856, but the Panic of 1857—a severe national financial crisis—depressed crop prices and caused bank failures and economic stagnation in Iowa.

Following the depression, forces beyond Iowa's borders were assembled that tore the nation apart. Questions about the abolition of slavery and states' rights provoked debate and controversy across the country. Some local residents, notably Isaac Brandt and Thomas Mitchell, were active abolitionists in the 1850s. They participated in the underground railroad, a secret system of safe houses for funneling former slaves to northern freedom. Brandt was a friend of John Brown, the eccentric leader of the ill-fated raid on Harper's Ferry.

The growing rift between North and South erupted in earnest in 1861, and Polk County residents shifted to a wartime economy and way of life. Few imagined in April 1861, when the Confederates fired on Fort Sumter in South Carolina, that the conflict would drag across four bloody years.

In the face of this national crisis, politicians and local leaders assembled to orate, organize, and profess their patriotism. Led by the stirring words of Marcellus M. Crocker, who rose to the rank of brigadier general in the Union Army, 100 men stepped forward "to go with

G.I. Reynolds, the artist of this panoramic view of Des Moines as seen from the new capitol, reportedly based his artwork on 1858 photographs. A few structures are identifiable, including the Walnut Street and Court Avenue bridges, and the mills along the Des Moines River. Courtesy, Barbara Beving Long

The Law Library in the capitol was to have had committee rooms above it, but the capitol commissioners thought otherwise. After seeing the library at Michigan's capitol, they devoted the space to library stacks, making a soaring 45-foot expanse for five tiers of books and a spiral staircase to reach them. Courtesy, State Historical Society of Iowa

In this rare photograph, the present capitol building is seen towering over the facility it replaced. The picture was taken from East 10th and Vine sometime in the late 1880s, before the earlier capitol burned. The Soldiers' and Sailors' Monument now occupies the old capitol site. Courtesy, State Historical Society of Iowa

[him] to Dixie." Less than a month later, Company D, Second Iowa Infantry Volunteers, formally enlisted at headquarters in Keokuk. Company D was the county's first, but assuredly not the last.

A total of 1,433 men and boys served in the Second Iowa Infantry Volunteers during the Civil War. Of that number 75 were killed, 24 died from wounds, and 121 succumbed to disease. Another 312 were wounded but survived, and 15 were captured. Such a distribution of casualties was not unusual. More men died from disease than from battlefield injuries in the Civil War.

Military service depopulated families and entire townships. Patriarch John B. Saylor acted as company sutler for the 23rd Iowa and kept an eye on his son-in-law and four sons. He explained: "I go to watch over the men of Saylor Township, and see that they want for nothing that can be got to them by my assistance." He died of disease at Vicksburg in 1863.

Iowans participated in most of the significant battles of the Civil War. Regiments raised in Polk County fought at Pea Ridge, Arkansas, and Fort Donelson and Shiloh, Tennessee. They fought at Vicksburg and Corinth, and marched to

the sea with General William Tecumseh Sherman (brother of Des Moines businessmen Hoyt and Lampson Sherman). Iowans crossed most Southern states, from Missouri to Virginia. They also pulled guard and prison duty, defended the state's western border from Indian threats, and were stationed at forts in the West, far from the sounds of battle.

At home Iowans followed news of the war and responded with nervous gaiety to reports of success. Meeting in an unusual extra session, the legislature heard of the Union capture of Fort Donelson when *Des Moines Register* editor Frank Palmer rushed in with the news.

Brigadier General Marcellus M. Crocker is recalled in Des Moines through the street named for him. Crocker, who received some training at West Point, rose quickly in the ranks from captian to brigadier general but died in 1865 at the age of 35. General U.S. Grant pronounced him "fit to command an independent army," a high compliment. Courtesy, State Historical Society of Iowa

The Second Iowa Infantry Volunteers, including Company D from Polk County, spent the winter of 1863 near Corinth. The usual camp diseases of the era, such as ague, brain fever, and consumption, were constant companions. Those who endured the rigors of camp life were among the ten Iowa infantry regiments that fought in the Battle of Corinth. Courtesy, State Historical Society of Iowa

On January 11, 1865, the 12 companies of the Second Iowa Cavalry camped at Eastport, Mississippi. This rare drawing was taken from a photograph and offers an unusual rendering of a Union cavalry camp. Snuggly nestled into a hillside, each company had its own row of housing consisting of log huts with canvas tops. The decorative arches at the ends of the rows may have been a morale-boosting, competitive exercise for the companies. Courtesy, State Historical Society of Iowa

Speaker Rush Clark "sprang to his feet, in the very midst of a roll call," recalled the house clerk, and shouted out the victory. The legislators were so enthused that they were unable to work and authorized a 34-round salute to be fired from Capitol Hill.

Speechmaking and celebrating were undoubtedly more pleasurable pastimes than grappling with the difficult problems besetting the state. Before the Civil War, Iowa had no militia in place and no arms, equipment, or funds to supply volunteers. During this period states had the responsibility for both recruiting and equipping soldiers.

Iowans worked together to provide clothing, supplies, and money for the needy. Iowa women organized a statewide network of Sanitary Commissions to provide hospital supplies. In Des Moines the Ladies' Soldiers' Aid Society held fund-raising festivals and concerts, netting $94 at their 1862 autumn concert. And the Soldiers' Families' Relief Association helped the families the soldiers left behind. In one three-month period in 1865 the group helped 79 needy families with monthly stipends of $10 to $25.

The war ended in April 1865, four years to the month after its start. Polk County residents set about adjusting to peacetime. Orphans, widows, and wounded veterans needed care. Businesses—especially the woolen mills and pork packers who supplied the army—readjusted to peacetime markets. Farm wives prepared to hand over farm duties to returning husbands. And new groups appeared on the political horizon to press their causes.

The years following the Civil War brought an organizational change in

The Civil War profoundly affected all segments of Iowa society. With husbands gone, women found themselves thrust into unfamiliar and solitary roles. Women were now responsible for running the farm and seeing to the crops and livestock in addition to their traditional duties. Women also helped in the war effort by rolling bandages and providing supplies for the front. Courtesy, State Historical Society of Iowa

the American political and social scene. Perhaps to bring order out of the chaos of a fratricidal war, groups of like-minded people established organizations to further their cause, a new idea at the time. In 1874 Iowa lawyers created the first state bar association west of the Mississippi and the second in the nation. Iowa farmers joined third-party movements such as the Greenback Party and cooperative societies such as the Patrons of Husbandry. Veterans, temperance advocates, and women all organized to press their particular causes. The late nineteenth-century political arena was a lively place indeed.

In the 1870s Polk County women led the state in the effort to extend the vote to women. Des Moines resident Annie Savery was among the founders, with Amelia Bloomer, of the Iowa Woman Suffrage Association in 1870. The same year Savery also helped found the Polk County Woman Suffrage Society, whose members faithfully held monthly meetings for 50 years.

Civil War veterans formed their own group to press their cause. First organized in 1866, the Grand Army of the Republic had 519 posts in Iowa and a peak membership of 52,013 in 1890. The Union Army veterans allied themselves with two potent forces: the railroads, who set the rates farmers paid to ship grain, and Des Moines journalist James S. Clarkson and his influential *Iowa State Register*. From the 1870s and into the 1890s this triumvirate of special interests, known as the Regency, dominated

The Soldiers' and Sailors' Monument, shown here under construction in 1895, remains the most prominent of the commemorative statuary in the capitol complex. It was built as a memorial to "all Iowa soldiers and sailors who engaged in the War of the Rebellion." Courtesy, State Historical Society of Iowa

The residence of Annie Savery is seen here in an image from the mid 1870s. Savery was an outspoken advocate of the suffrage movement and one of the founders of the Iowa Woman Suffrage Association in 1870. According to one of several laudatory obituaries, Savery was a talented intellectual, "naturally brilliant and forceful" with "a social grace and power that was extraordinary." Courtesy, Des Moines Pioneer Club

Republican party politics and, by extension, state government. Opposition to the Regency's power prompted Iowans to join new organizations and new political parties in the 1870s.

The Patrons of Husbandry was not conceived as a political party, but the group did exert pressure on the legislature. The Patrons of Husbandry (or Grangers) was a secret fraternal organization for farmers that sought regulation of the railroads and the often exorbitant rates they charged. Granges, the local units of the Patrons of Husbandry, also offered a variety of self-help programs, such as cooperative purchase and sale of farm machinery and farm products. In 1873, when a national financial panic closed banks and caused hardship on the farms, Iowa had more Granges (1,507) than any other state. Polk County farmers organized 30 of them.

In February 1873, 1,200 delegates representing some 50,000 Iowa Grangers converged upon Des Moines to demand passage of a rate law to protect them from the railroads' price-gouging. The Iowa City *Daily Press* termed it the "largest indoor gathering ever held in the state." Legislators listened to them and passed the first of many railroad rate restrictions in Iowa.

Yet another group, the temperance forces, added to the heady mixture of third-party politics in the late nineteenth century. By the 1870s prohibitionists were actively involved in efforts to limit the sale, production, and use of intoxicating beverages. In the 1880s Iowans passed a state constitutional amendment prohibiting the use of alcohol. The chief casualties were local breweries and the International Distillery in Des Moines, which processed corn into alcohol for export to Europe.

Establishment of a government system for regulating and protecting citizens and their property was one of the first acts taken on by residents in the

When James Long ran the Avenue House in 1866, he boasted that "no liquor bar disgraces the House." During the Civil War, the Avenue House was an enlistment headquarters. By the time of this photograph, the 1870s, several additions had been made to the hotel, and a number of proprietors had operated it. It was located on the south side of Court Avenue between Third and Fourth streets. Courtesy, Des Moines Pioneer Club

The patrons of J. Christian Hansen's saloon raise their glasses of beer. Hansen's saloon was located on the east side from the late 1890s, after repeal of Prohibition in 1894, into the early 1900s. Hansen is shown at right behind the bar. Courtesy, Des Moines Pioneer Club

area west of the Red Rock Line. Men (women could not yet vote) set about organizing systems of government at the local level. These organizational activities began in 1845, with the end of military jurisdiction, and culminated in 1857 when the state capital moved to Des Moines.

Acquisition of the state capital in the 1850s brought the new city of Des Moines unparalleled growth, making it the political, population, and approximate geographical center of Iowa. An 1856 guidebook noted that the new capital "has been almost besieged by lawyers, doctors, agents and land speculators." Population increased accordingly, from 502 in 1850 to 3,800 six years later. The city prepared to attain another leading role, that of the commercial center of the state.

Employees of Waldron Brothers display some of their products in this photograph from the 1870s. Abraham and George Waldron built a foundry and machine works in Des Moines in 1873. By 1875 they had 80 employees. Courtesy, Des Moines Pioneer Club

CHAPTER FOUR

An Enterprising Place

Shacks and other crude buildings dating from before the Civil War were, according to a contemporary news account, "as thick as toadstools on Walnut Street from the bridge to the Exposition building, and also abounded on Third and Fourth streets and Sixth and Seventh." That was the appearance of much of downtown Des Moines in 1880. But in just five years, three-, four-, and even five-story brick blocks replaced the early modest buildings, cheap billboards, and stands of cottonwood trees. Des Moines enjoyed its first great building boom in the 1880s, its first sustained brush with prosperity.

A visitor returning after just five years would not have recognized the place in 1885. Commercial enterprise now extended on the west side from Court Avenue to Walnut and Locust streets and stretched as far west from the river as Twelfth Street. The proud Globe, Eagle, and Rogg-Detchon blocks replaced hastily built wood frame buildings between Fourth and Fifth on Walnut. In the next block every building but one was new or had been rebuilt since 1880, including Younkers store and the Des Moines National Bank. Thirty-seven new business blocks and 725 residences went up in 1881 alone.

By 1885 the Capital City had finally surpassed the older Mississippi River towns in population. Boosters trumpeted the news: Des Moines ranked fifth in the state in 1875, but soared to first place in just 10 years. This burgeoning population reached 22,408 in 1880 and swelled to 62,139 by 1900.

Blessed with excellent railroad connections, Des Moines became the statewide center for wholesaling. Traveling salesmen or runners rode the rails to visit customers in the hinterland and take orders. By 1890 the wholesale houses had 416 runners throughout the state, and the number grew to 1,300 by 1920. Wholesalers of groceries, builders' supplies, printing and paper supplies, and farm implements built large warehouses near the tracks south of and along Court Avenue.

This drawing from 1889 shows the north side of Walnut Street, looking east from Fifth to Fourth streets. Just beyond Fifth Street are the Globe block and the Eagle block with its ornate cornice. Osgood, Harris & Company, touted as "the largest dry goods house in the city," was located across the alley from the Eagle block. From Des Moines City Directory, *1889*

Des Moines was also the center for retailing, including the newest type of shopping place, the department store. The rise of the modern department store had its roots in France in 1852; in Des Moines Mandelbaum's, Harris-Emery, Younkers, and Wilkins' were leading examples of this innovation. The small, old-style dry goods stores relied on high markups, low service, and goods jumbled together, generally on a single floor in a narrow storefront shop. The grand new department store was an imposing, multi-storied rectangular shape; merchandise was spread throughout in carefully arranged departments. Large plate glass windows filled with merchandise enticed passersby. Inside, elevators carried customers aloft where an army of clerks stood ready to assist. Browsing was encouraged, and returns or exchanges allowed—new ideas all.

Younkers' evolution to the largest and most prominent retail chain in the state began modestly enough in 1856 in the river town of Keokuk when Lipman, Samuel, and Marcus Younker opened a small store. Realizing that Des Moines was a growing city, a younger Younker brother, Herman, opened a branch operation which became the principal store in 1874. Ever the innovator, in 1880 Younkers was the first store in Iowa to employ a woman as a salesclerk. By 1893 the store had no less than 50 clerks.

Beginning in 1873 the brothers Isaac and Jeheil Tone manufactured and sold ground spices, coffees, and baking powder to Iowa cooks. They later said they had to educate Iowans to appreciate the taste of roasted coffee. They were apparently successful in that endeavor, for by 1888 they offered Ribera, Ambrosia, Royal, Golden, Tacoma, and Cosmos brands of coffee. Courtesy, Des Moines Pioneer Club

This photograph from 1879 shows a group of workers outside George Lunn's paint shop on Sixth Street. George Lunn is standing to the right of the entrance. The workman on the left displays a wallpaper sample, and another appears to be holding a paint can and brush. Courtesy, Des Moines Pioneer Club

In 1899 the Younker brothers opened their present department store at Seventh and Walnut streets in the heart of the retail district. Of the four department stores once clustered there, only Younkers has survived.

While commercial expansion brought Des Moines and Polk County statewide recognition, locally founded insurance companies vaulted the Capital City to national eminence. As early as 1883, Des Moines was known as the "Hartford of

The sumptuous interior of Terrace Hill accurately reflected the wealth Frederick M. Hubbell amassed. The finest materials were used throughout the home, including rosewood handrails, burl veneered doors, and walnut, butternut and oak trim. Hubbell, who became the richest man in Iowa, bought the magnificent Victorian mansion in 1884. Courtesy, Iowa Bureau of Historic Preservation

the West." Boosters claimed that more money was invested in insurance in Des Moines than in any other city west of the Mississippi.

The career of F.M. Hubbell was synonymous with insurance and wealth in Des Moines. From his beginnings in 1855 as a humble but ambitious clerk in Des Moines, Hubbell went on to found Equitable Life Insurance Company of Iowa in 1867 and to amass one of Iowa's largest fortunes. Equitable of Iowa, as it is known, remains a prosperous force in the insurance industry.

By 1888, 11 insurance companies with combined assets of $2,643,974 had their home offices in Des Moines. By 1910 the number had grown to 44, and Des Moines was clearly the leading insurance center in the country after Hartford, Connecticut. Des Moines-based companies insured against tornado and hail damage as well as the more common disasters of fire and death.

Private, state, and national banks, building and loan societies, loan and trust companies, and, later, savings and loan associations, provided an additional layer of

AN ENTERPRISING PLACE

49

Even in the 1940s the Equitable Building towered over its neighbors. Completed in 1924, the 18-story office building featured a polished granite base, brick upper stories, and a creamy terra cotta cornice. It is a fitting monument to the financial strength of Equitable of Iowa. Gothic Revival tracery and its size make it among the city's most distinctive buildings. Courtesy, Des Moines Pioneer Club

financial strength for Des Moines and Polk County. In the post-Civil War years Des Moines emerged as Iowa's financial center, a position it has retained.

The earliest banks in Des Moines were private ventures. No federal or state agencies protected depositors, and no national banking system regulated currency values. Early influential bankers included Hoyt Sherman, who with P.M. Casady, R.L. Tidrick, and B.F. Allen established Hoyt Sherman and Company. But even their combined expertise and influence could not prevent failures during the financial Panic of 1857 that swept the nation.

One result of this devastating panic that most Iowa banks did not survive was a stronger and more diverse banking system, including state and national banks. By 1888 Des Moines was host to five national, one state, and four savings banks. There were also a number of loan and trust companies, of which Iowa Loan & Trust Company was the most prominent.

The first newspaper in Polk County, the *Iowa Star*, dated from 1849 and was fol-

Citizens' National Bank, one of the city's most prominent banks, was organized in 1873 and established operations in the new Clapp Block. Located at the southwest corner of Fifth and Walnut streets, the building sustained heavy fire damage on January 11, 1883. Despite the burnt, ice-laden appearance of the building, the bank was able to open for business the next day, its vaults intact. Courtesy, Des Moines Pioneer Club

lowed soon after by Lampson Sherman's *Fort Des Moines Gazette*. Thirst for contact with the outside world and the urge to unite under a political banner were behind establishment of more than one newspaper. Early newspapers were openly and fiercely partisan. Thus, even a community as small as Fort Des Moines in the 1840s sponsored two publications. The *Iowa Star* spoke for the Democratic party while the rival *Gazette* represented the Whigs.

Des Moines' prominence as state capital and the accompanying political activities of the legislature drew newspapermen to the city. The 1870 arrival of the Clarkson family—patriarch Coker and brothers Richard and James S.—heralded the beginning of "The Newspaper Iowa Depends Upon," the present *Des Moines Register*. The Clarksons bought the *Iowa State Register* and doubled its circulation by 1885. A new technology, the Linotype machine, allowed larger newspapers and increasingly elaborate advertising, and the population boom brought increased readership.

The 30-year Clarkson era ended with the century. New editors and owners of the by-then *Register & Leader*, Harvey Ingham and Gardner Cowles, Sr., combined keen journalistic ability with sound business judgment. Their newspaper achieved statewide readership and took on modern trappings. Ingham and Cowles instituted new sports, amusement, and picture sections and expanded existing departments. They hired an excellent staff, including Pulitzer Prize-winning political cartoonist Jay N. "Ding" Darling. Circulation rose dramatically, and by 1911 the paper was the 17th-largest west of the Mississippi. Statewide domination accelerated in the following decades; the *Sunday Register* reached an astonishing 70 percent of Iowa households in 1940.

Given Des Moines' place amid some of the best farmland in the world, establishment of farm journals was an obvious and welcome development. Although farm journals dated from the 1850s in Iowa, their key period began in the 1870s when journals began advocating "book farming," the study and application of proven agricultural practices. Des Moines was home for three highly influential journals, the *Iowa Homestead*, *Wallaces' Farmer*, and *Successful Farming*.

The Wallace family's dominance in agriculture spread beyond the printed word. In 1926 Henry A. Wallace was the first to breed and market hybrid seed corn on a commercial scale. Within 10 years Pioneer Hi-Bred International was (and remains) a resounding success. Wallace also served in the administrations of Warren G. Harding, Franklin D. Roosevelt, and Harry S. Truman. He almost became president. Wallace was vice president under Roosevelt, but his increasingly outspoken views met with

Beginning his newspaper career in 1866 as a compositor or typesetter, James S. Clarkson was editor of the influential Iowa State Register between 1870 and 1891. He combined journalism with Republican politics, serving as chairman of the Republican State Committee. Clarkson also held national posts in the Republican Party and received several governmental appointments. Courtesy, State Historical Society of Iowa

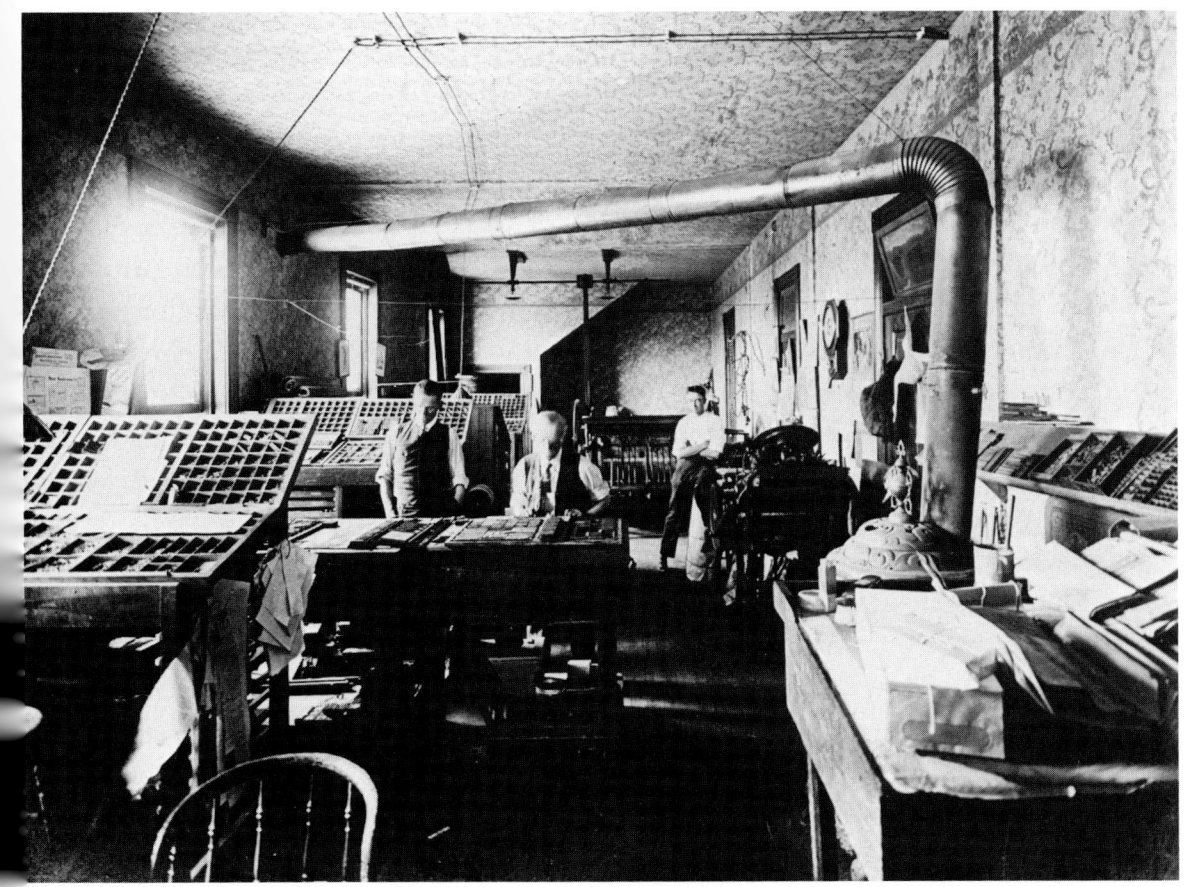

Even the small town of Mitchellville had its own newspaper. E.P. Marmon founded the Mitchellville Index *in 1882 and guided its development until his death in 1913. Henry Marmon, shown here with his printer's devil and son Charles perched on a roll of paper, then took over. The* Index *remained in the Marmon family until 1934, when the Altoona* Herald *bought it. Courtesy, Mary Marmon*

In his nearly 50 year career with the Des Moines Register, Pulitzer prize winner Jay N. "Ding" Darling drew around 15,000 cartoons. One of America's best known cartoonists, Darling was also known for his commitment to conservation. A wildlife refuge is named for him in Florida. Darling is pictured on the left in this photo from the 1920s. The nickname "Ding" is actually "D'ing," a contraction of Darling. Courtesy, Des Moines Pioneer Club

disapproval in the White House. Truman was tapped to replace him on the 1944 ticket and became president upon Roosevelt's death.

Polk County's location in farming country spawned other farm-related enterprise. By 1881, 16 agricultural implement dealers in Des Moines served area farmers, and surrounding towns also had dealers in John Deere plows, rotary disk corn planters, and McCormick's harvesting machines. Carriage works, saddlers, and harness-makers saw to the needs of both town and country clientele. The Des Moines Saddlery Company, whose renovated building still stands on Court Avenue, built the lofty structure in the 1880s. There they made 55 different grades of harnesses, saddles, horse collars, and leather fly nets.

George C. Baker made "Baker Perfect" barbed wire, the only version that neared the sales volume and popularity of the nation's most successful version, J.F. Glidden's "Winner" wire. Iowans favored the homegrown version all the more when editorials in the *Iowa Homestead* and the *State Register* condemned the Glidden monopoly during the patent litigation of the 1870s.

The Central Oil Works, whose factory still stands on East Fourth Street, processed flax seed into linseed oil for export beginning in 1866. Shannon and Mott's Des Moines Roller Mills marketed several brands of flour, including Falcon and Neola, and a special pancake flour. The latter was only available during the "pancake season," from September to May.

Purveyors of patent medicine, cosmetics, and grooming products brought a flair to Des Moines manufacturing. Lowell and Davis S. Chamberlain began making Chamberlain Cough Syrup and Chamberlain's Colic, Cholera and Diarrhea Remedy in Des Moines in 1881. One of their salesmen, Will A. Peairs, extended his territory to Hawaii, then to Alaska and Mexico, reaching South Africa in 1894.

A nephew of the Chamberlains, Carl Weeks, started out selling Weeks' Break Up a Cold Tablet. Like the Chamberlains, however, he moved from rather suspect patent medicines into the realm of good grooming. In 1915 he began marketing Armand Cold Cream Face Powder. Packaged in a distinctive pink and white box, it was the best-selling powder in America in the 1920s. By 1934 the company had a line of 275 cosmetics available in 45,000 stores across the country.

F.W. Fitch also reached a national market, especially through "The Fitch Bandwagon." The musical radio program was among the most popular in the 1930s and 1940s. Everyone from Jack Benny to Cab Calloway to the Andrews Sisters entertained listeners, who were urged to buy the company's Ideal Dandruff Remover.

Polk County lay in the center of the state's largest band of coal deposits. Coal was so plentiful that Captain James Allen authorized A.N. Hayes, a civilian attached to the army contingent, to scratch it out of the exposed riverbanks in 1843 to warm the dragoons of Fort

Established in 1902, the cannery at Grimes was a Polk County industry directly related to agriculture. During the sweet corn season, the plant ran day and night. Jessie Bohrofen and Sarah Hammond behind her are shown at the closing machine around 1910. Other workers shucked corn and placed can lids by hand. Courtesy, Reverend and Mrs. Harry F. Stickle

In 1866, 25,321 sheep scampered over Polk County farms. Their owners reaped 84,970 pounds of wool from them. Much of that wool was brought to the Shepard, Perrior & Bennett City Mill. Shown here in the 1860s, the woolen mill was located on the site of the present Des Moines Municipal Building at East First and Locust. Courtesy, Des Moines Pioneer Club

Des Moines No. 2. Hall's Coal Bank of 1850 was probably the first nonmilitary coal mine, but the title of the most persistent coal miner went to Wesley Redhead. The Englishman began his quest for a good mine in 1864. Nine years later he found it, a rich vein four feet thick at the south end of the Seventh Street bridge.

Redhead's Des Moines Coal Company inaugurated large-scale coal mining in Polk County. An increasing population required an inexpensive heating source. Also, locomotives on the many rail lines crossing the county needed stoking, so "shipping mines" proliferated in the 1870s. Mine owners located shafts near the lines—it was that easy to find a coal seam.

Much of Des Moines, especially the east, north, and south sides, is underlaid with old coal mines. Occasionally a street collapses into a former shaft or part of a yard unaccountably sinks, reminders of the once thriving operations. In the 1880s the Watson Coal Company employed 44 miners to take 50 tons a day from the mine at East 15th Street and the Rock Island Railroad tracks. George Garver's Giant Mine #2 was located at East 20th and Grand Avenue in 1883, now a quiet residential area.

With every decade coal production increased in the county. The peak years ran from 1908 to 1920, when average annual production reached a phenomenal 1,500,000 tons. The 15 to 20 mines just

Until the 1950s, one of Des Moines' most famous companies was undoubtedly the F.W. Fitch Company. The firm was known worldwide for its Fitch Dandruff Remover Shampoo. They were also known through the top-rated Fitch Bandwagon, a radio show heard Sunday evenings on NBC. Courtesy, Denny Rehder

The Des Moines based architectural firm of Smith & Keffer designed the O'Brien County Courthouse (the plans to which can be seen in the foreground), the Public Library of Des Moines, several Des Moines schools, and a number of buildings on the Iowa State Fairgrounds. The firm of Keffer & Jones succeeded Smith & Keffer in 1916 and is represented here by Karl K. Keffer, at left, and Earl E. Jones. Courtesy, Karl Keffer Associates, P.C., Architects

in Des Moines employed 2,943 miners in 1910. Polk County ranked as the state's second-largest coal producer for 50 years.

As mines were played out close to Des Moines, mining companies moved into the countryside. They established large mining camps such as Oralabor, Marquisville, Carney, Enterprise, Norwoodville, and Carbondale. When a mine closed, the owners moved operations, including mine tipples, shacks, and housing, on to the next shaft. The now middle-class areas of Windsor Heights, Beaverdale, and Valley Junction were once sites of coal mining.

In 1889 the Carbondale Coal Company opened a shaft three miles south-

Wesley Redhead's South Park Mine opened in 1873, two years before this rarely seen photograph was taken. The rich vein of coal, over four feet thick, was not played out for 20 years. By 1876 150 miners worked the subterranean mine. Courtesy, Des Moines Pioneer Club

Yugoslavians from the state of Croatia joined other immigrants in the mines around Polk County. They are shown here at the Norwood White Coal Company Mine No. 8 in 1939. Note the traditional miner's aluminum lunch buckets which held food in the top compartment and coffee or water below. Courtesy, Croatian Fraternal Slavic Center

east of the fairgrounds near the Wabash Railroad. For nearly 20 years the area, now part of the Des Moines suburb of Pleasant Hill, was home for boarders in four boardinghouses and for some 175 mining families. Many were Swedish immigrants, with such names as Grandquist, Erickson, and Gustafson.

The miners lived at the mercy of the mine owners. They bought at the company store using coupon books and the company doctor attended to them for a monthly fee. The company also owned the houses of Carbondale and rented the three- or four-room homes for six or eight dollars a month. Perched on wood blocks, the modest wood-frame dwellings lacked central heating, plumbing, and electricity.

Unsafe working conditions and long hours for miserable pay led workers to organize unions. In 1899 Polk County miners established District 13 of the United Mine Workers (UMW). By 1910 conditions had improved considerably. No longer did miners spend 11 or 12 hours in the mines. The eight-hour day was standard. Wages had increased by 30 percent since 1899. Working conditions also improved, with better ventilation and regulated use of blasting powder. District 13 maintained a fund to pay benefits to disabled miners and death benefits to their widows; $65,317 was paid out between 1906 and early 1910.

The 1880s brought unparalleled prosperity to all sectors of the county's economy, with much of the growth concentrated in Des Moines. Having achieved a leading economic position, county residents still had to weather the financial doldrums of the 1890s. The Panic of 1893 affected all categories of commercial enterprise. Many of the businesses begun so optimistically in the 1880s failed to survive the following decade.

But new ones, many based on new technologies and ways of living, emerged to replace them. As the largest city in Iowa, Des Moines naturally evolved as the principal place for automobile-related busi-

Among the many specialized shops in Des Moines during the 1880s was Estey & Camp at 502 Walnut Street. The firm sold musical instruments, sheet music, pianos, and organs. William H. Leyman, the store manager during this period, was also the man who composed the "Des Moines City Waltz." Courtesy, Des Moines Pioneer Cub

Visitors to Lozier's "Mammoth New Greenhouses" around the turn of the century were amazed at the botanical splendor beneath 40,000 square feet of glass. Isaac W. Lozier boasted that he took all the first premiums at the Iowa State Fair for his flowers. Lozier's started modestly in the 1880s, but by 1895 offered fine plants from two Des Moines locations. Courtesy, State Historical Society of Iowa

Des Moines merchants Ross and Ashton Clemens opened an automobile dealership in this six-story building in 1916 at Tenth and Mulberry. The building was specifically designed to accommodate the weight of cars stored on the upper floors. Courtesy, Barbara Beving Long

nesses. In 1907 there were already five auto showrooms offering 17 types of cars, and one factory, the Mason Motor Car Company.

Just three years later, 18 auto dealers displayed an incredible 125 styles of automobiles at the first auto show in Des Moines. An estimated 16,000 people paid 25 cents apiece to attend. Festivities began with a parade involving over 150 car owners traveling at a brisk 17 miles per hour. Popular cornetist and band leader T. Fred Henry penned the "Auto Show March" for the occasion. In conjunction with the show, Governor B.F. Carroll sponsored the first state convention on the problems of road maintenance.

Des Moines residents, enamored of the automobile, sought to make central Iowa a center for the emerging automobile industry. Edward R. Mason, an attorney, invested in Fred Duesenberg's Mason Motor Car, marking the first significant automobile manufacturing in Des Moines. Known as the "Hill Climber" for its ability to climb the statehouse steps with ease, around 1,750 cars were produced between 1905 and 1910. Duesenberg was responsible for its design and fabrication. He later achieved worldwide recognition for the Duesenberg, an automobile that set the standard for speed and luxury.

Patterns of commercial and financial leadership from the 1880s solidified in the early twentieth century. Like the prosperity of the 1880s, the growth and development of the 1920s changed the face of Des Moines, adding multi-story buildings downtown and acres of new subdivisions across the city. Shoppers in 1927 could choose from 5 department stores, 46 auto dealers, and 225 filling stations. Wholesaling accounted for $152,314,064 of business, $18,540,600 of that from automobile and accessories sales. With 15 banks having $62,784,292 in deposits and some 40 insurance companies with a total annual income of over $100 million in 1927, the city likewise retained its solid financial standing.

With the coming of the twentieth century, Des Moines stood secure—but not stagnant—as the dominant city in Iowa. Further political and social change was on the horizon. Renewed prosperity and technological advances brought ever more consumer goods and significantly altered the way Iowans lived and viewed the world beyond its borders. New immigrant groups arrived to contribute to the cultural mosaic of the county.

AN ENTERPRISING PLACE

The Mason Motor Car, shown here at the 1909 Iowa State Fair, was famous for its ability to climb steep inclines. Ed Mason, the owner of the automobile factory that bore his name, is seated on the left front seat of the light-colored car. Courtesy, State Historical Society of Iowa

Proving itself as the "Hill Climber," a 1908 Mason automobile tackles the Capitol steps with its mighty two-cylinder engine. Perceptions about the horseless carriage changed as it became increasingly familiar. The automobile was initially regarded as but a sideshow curiosity, then an expensive toy good only for racing, and finally as an important mode of transportation. Courtesy, State Historical Society of Iowa

The C.C. Taft Company specialized in wholesale produce and cigars, using this truck to make deliveries. Courtesy, Barbara Beving Long

CHAPTER FIVE

Changes with the New Century

"Our new home has many advantages over the old one, and I like it much better . . . when I compare Sweden with this country, I have no desire to return," wrote Iowa settler Mary Stephenson in 1864. Lithuanian Jew Saul Davidson, remembering his days as a peddler in the 1880s before he settled in Des Moines to establish Iowa's largest furniture store, said, "It was hard. I could speak no English. I would go from farm to farm, peddling my goods. Often I would walk 15 miles a day." And about his 1910 arrival in Des Moines, Croatian-born John Liker recalled, "What I made in one week [here], I had to work for a whole month [to earn in Yugoslavia]."

Immigrants to America left their native lands for a variety of reasons, but the paramount motivation was economic. New arrivals sought a better life and increased religious, economic, and social freedoms. Successive waves of immigrants from Northern Europe and then from Southern and Central Europe produced a cultural patchwork quilt in Iowa and Polk County that has enriched our society. Despite this influx of nationalities, the American-born populace far outnumbered other nationalities in Polk County. In 1895, 62,981 of the county's 72,888 residents had been born in America. However, many of these were children of immigrants.

The Irish were the first to emigrate to this country in large numbers, beginning in the first half of the nineteenth century. In Polk County 3,549 residents hailed from Canada, England, Ireland, Scotland, and Wales, according to the 1895 state census. Thus most area residents spoke English, which made assimilation into the community an easier task. Other immigrant groups needed to master English before embarking on the road to cherished economic success.

German-speaking residents made up another important early immigrant group in mid-nineteenth century Polk County. Like those who came later, they established their own institutions—churches, newspapers, and schools —that paralleled English-speaking institutions. In the 1870s

German-Jewish immigrants built the first synagogue in Des Moines in 1887 at Eighth and Pleasant streets. Orthodox congregations were organized in 1876 (Congregation B'nai Israel) and 1881 (Beth El Jacob) to serve the mostly Southern and Eastern European immigrants who initially settled on the city's east side. In 1901 reform-minded Eastern European Jews organized Tifereth Israel. Courtesy, Des Moines Pioneer Club

Germans established the first German language newspaper in Des Moines, the *Iowa Staats Anzeiger*. As late as 1914, the *Anzeiger* flourished, still printed in German, under the longtime editorship of Joseph Eiboeck.

Germans in Polk County were Protestant, Catholic, and Jewish. The first Jewish resident in the county was Wilhelm Krauss, who opened a dry goods store in 1845. He used one of the former log cabins of the second Fort Des Moines. By 1869 Des Moines' Jewish population totaled around 35. Many operated retail and wholesale businesses, having begun their mercantile career as peddlers canvassing the countryside.

By 1872 there were sufficient residents to support Des Moines' first Jewish congregation, B'nai Jeshurun. But it was in the 1880s that significant Jewish immigration occurred. In 1881 the county had around 250 Jews; by 1895 there were 1,100. The number of Jewish-owned businesses increased similarly, from 30 to 140. Most of these more recent immigrants came from Southern and Eastern European countries. Many were Orthodox Jews, unlike the German-born Reform Jews who had settled in Des Moines before them.

The first group of blacks to settle in Des Moines came in the 1860s. Jefferson Logan led a group of 13 former slaves from Missouri. However, the number of blacks in the county remained low. In 1880 the county was only 1.5 percent black, a figure that grew to 2.7 percent in 1900 and 4.3 percent in 1920.

Like other groups in Polk County, blacks organized their own institutions, including churches, fraternal orders, and newspapers. But these organizations carried a special urgency, since blacks were generally denied access to white institutions or were required to accept second-rate conditions. Living in a segregated society, black residents opened their own hotels, funeral parlors, barber shops, and restaurants. Renowned musicians such as Cab Calloway and Ethel Waters stayed at Nellie and Arthur Esters' place, La Margarita Hotel, at 1410 Center Street in the 1920s.

One of the most influential black institutions in Des Moines was the *Iowa Bystander*, established in 1894. There was a series of owners until J.B. Morris, Sr., bought the newspaper in the 1920s.

During Morris' 50 years of leadership, the *Bystander* was a beacon for black pride and a major voice for the black community.

Morris combined his editorial duties with a legal career. A number of other black leaders in Des Moines were also lawyers, including S. Joe Brown, George H. Woodson, and Gertrude Rush. When he graduated from the University of Iowa, Brown was the first black to receive a Phi Beta Kappa key west of the Mississippi—the 11th black in the country to receive this honor. In 1918 Rush became the first black woman to pass the Iowa Bar examination. The influence of black Des Moines lawyers was national. In 1907 Woodson, with Morris, Rush, Brown, and Charles Howard, organized a separate bar association for black Iowa lawyers. The organization was the direct forerunner of the National Bar Association established in the late 1920s; Woodson was its first president. The American Bar Association did not then admit blacks.

A host of European countries added to the immigration tide after the 1880s, including Sweden, Norway, and Denmark. By 1885 the 2,246 Scandinavian immigrants from these three countries surpassed the number of Germans (1,871) and Irish (1,547) in the county.

Arriving in 1862, Jefferson Logan was among the first former slaves to settle in Des Moines. He later held patronage jobs in the state capitol where his "possum suppers" were a favorite of legislators and governors. Courtesy, State Historical Society of Iowa

Black entrepreneur Robert N. Hyde got his start as an inventor and businessman while part of the cleaning staff at the Kirkwood Hotel. There he devised a particularly effective cleaning compound. Together with T.W. Henry, Hyde soon patented and marketed H. and H. brand soap for household cleaning use. H. and H. soap was still marketed as late as 1968. Courtesy, Des Moines Pioneer Club

Egidio Romano emigrated from Italy in 1889 and came to Des Moines three years later. He opened this fruit stand, with its delectable bunches of bananas and hot roasted peanuts, in a cranny of the Tuttle Building at Fifth and Walnut. A few years later, Romano, Joseph and Marco Chiesa, and Peter Dapolonia founded the Italian Importing Company. Not only did the company import such exotic delights as Italian bitters, Reggino and Pecorino cheeses, and macaroni, it also helped other Italians make the transition from Italy to America. Courtesy, Des Moines Pioneer Club

The Swedes were most numerous with 1,608 people. Like all the immigrant groups, they immediately set about establishing their own institutions, especially churches. Religious dissent concerning questions of liturgy and Biblical interpretations—and the intolerance it provoked—ranked high among the reasons Scandinavians chose to leave their homelands. Representatives of various sects and religions organized their own congregations, such as the Evangelical Covenant Church and the Swedish Evangelical Free Church, in Polk County. The first Swedish congregation was First Evangelical Lutheran Church, organized in 1869. The site of the present church at East Fifth and Des Moines streets clearly reflects the location of original settlement of Swedes in Des Moines on the east side near the river.

The Italians also contributed to the cultural mosaic of turn-of-the-century Polk County. Beginning with umbrella repairman Louis Jacopetti in 1880, Italians came to Polk County in increasing numbers. By 1915 an estimated 4,000 Italians worked in the coal mines and brickyards and on the railroads. Still others ran small grocery stores, fruit stands, and saloons, and operated pasta factories and bakeries.

Italians first settled in the lowland south of Court Avenue, amid railroad hotels, tracks, and depots, small factories, and wholesale houses, especially around S.W. 6th and Elm streets. Joseph Chiesa, originally a fruit seller, and Peter Dapolonia, who started out as a shoemaker, led the move to the second and current area of Italian settlement in Des Moines. When they could afford to, Italian families followed the streetcar line and moved to the south side of town across the Raccoon River. In the early 1900s St. Anthony's Catholic Church, Balistrieri's macaroni

factory, and Disalva's grocery/lodge hall served the neighborhood. Italian homes were recognizable by the large vegetable gardens, raised grape arbors, and outdoor bread ovens.

The bushel of nationalities that comprised Polk County was confronted with what must have seemed like an overwhelming array of changes. Not only was there a new language to learn, there were new technologies and ways of living in the early twentieth century. For those who could afford them, electrically powered vacuum cleaners, toasters, refrigerators, and washing machines eased domestic burdens dramatically. Three-pound electric irons replaced the up to 12-pound oven-heated flatirons.

Many households could afford to purchase these labor-saving devices. The period from 1900 to 1918 was a golden era of prosperity in Iowa. Crop prices were high and so was demand. Polk County farmers, and by extension city dwellers, enjoyed an unprecedented degree of affluence at the turn of the century.

Rural and urban residents built new homes, replacing picturesque Victorian styles with the clapboard and shingle of the Craftsman style, the sedate columns and pediments of the Colonial Revival style, and, less frequently, the horizontal lines and broad overhangs of the Prairie School. The countryside was peppered with new Four-Square houses, their hipped-roof, two-story boxy shapes a familiar sight. In Des Moines, the Craftsman style was especially popular, and developers built block upon block of houses featuring golden oak woodwork and cozy brick fireplaces. Some of the better versions had built-in vacuum systems, special nooks for milk delivery, and attached garages.

Among the new technologies which arose at the turn of the century was

Boarding houses such as the Skandinavisk Boarding House at 207 East Second Street were often the first homes for Scandinavian immigrants in Des Moines. The first substantial settlement of Scandinavians was located in the inexpensive riverside lowlands of the east side in the 1880s. Modest wood frame houses were found along the Des Moines River from Scott Avenue to East Court Avenue and also near Des Moines Street. As the immigrants became more prosperous around the turn of the century, they moved to the less flood-prone areas around East Sixth and East Ninth. The area was known as "Scandia Hill". Courtesy, Des Moines Pioneer Club

In addition to establishing a number of steam railroads out of Des Moines, Jefferson Polk was also responsible for popularizing the interurban in central Iowa and for consolidating Des Moines' streetcar systems. Harry H. Polk, Jefferson's son, was president and general manager of the Interurban Railway Company in the 1900s. The interurbans made travel to and within Des Moines convenient. A night on the town before catching the last interurban to Altoona, for example, became a reasonable possiblity. The approximately ten-mile journey took about fifty minutes. From As We See 'Em, Des Moines, Iowa.

At the turn of the century the interurban railway brought an alternative to steam-powered railroads. The interurbans carried shoppers and salesmen to town, miners to work, and even hauled milk from farms to the creamery. Courtesy, Collection of Ronald D. Sims

the electrically powered interurban railway. The quieter, cleaner, and cheaper interurbans supplemented and sometimes replaced steam railroads, once the salvation of Iowa communities. The interurbans carried rural residents to Des Moines shops and traveling salesmen out to their territories. Tourists boarded interurbans bound for the health baths and mineral waters at Colfax, a popular resort in nearby Jasper County. Miners commuted to the mine, teachers and students rode to classes, and farmers hauled milk to the creamery—such were the diverse uses of the newest transportation technology.

Beginning in the late 1890s, electric railway lines extended to newly developing Des Moines suburbs, such as Valley Junction (1898) and Urbandale (1904). They connected with Altoona and Mitchellville on the way to Colfax, and with Ankeny, Alleman, and a series of mining towns on a northerly route. On the way to Perry the interurbans brought soldiers and visitors to Johnston, site of Camp Dodge in World War I. There was also an interurban to the third and present Fort Des Moines on Army Post Road beginning in 1902.

From the late 1890s into the 1940s, interurbans across the county provided an attractive alternative to the grime and cost of steam railroad travel. But an even more alluring alternative was in the offing: the motor vehicle. More

Des Moines had its share of automobile makers at the turn of the century, including George G. Eldridge. Out of his machine shop, shown here at 117-119 Grand Avenue, Eldridge built one automobile and several trucks as early as 1903. Courtesy, Barbara Beving Long

than any other state, Iowans took to this latest transportation innovation in record numbers. In 1915 Iowa led the nation in the ratios of both population and driver-age persons to number of registered vehicles. Iowans continued to purchase from the bewildering variety of automobiles in record numbers, retaining the number one ranking into the 1920s.

The gasoline engine changed rural life immeasurably, ending isolation by shortening travel time. The automobile allowed farm families to spend far less time reaching church, school, or stores. The truck speeded the delivery of grain and livestock to market. The tractor and other motor-driven equipment revolutionized farming, which then required less manpower to grow and harvest the same amount of crops.

The lure of the motor vehicle proved irresistible and farmers became the largest buyers of cars and trucks and the strongest promoters of good roads. By 1922 Des Moines boosters were working to ease downtown traffic congestion and parking problems. And in 1927, Iowa at last began to pave its roads, gaining the first completely paved, cross-state road three years later. Iowa was coming "out of the mud."

Turn of-the-century changes in Polk County were not confined to acquiring new products and laborsaving devices. In the 1900s Des Moines residents took

CHANGES WITH THE NEW CENTURY

steps that led to a dramatic change in their form of government in 1907, and gained national recognition for their reforms. Known as the Des Moines Plan, the system was based on an elected mayor and four commissioners who were each responsible for city departments: streets and public improvements, parks and public property, public affairs and public safety, and accounts and finance.

Des Moines in the 1900s was governed better than many American cities. That is not to say there were no problems. In a campaign to improve the city, local newspapers described the "streets encumbered by refuse," a dilapidated riverfront, red light districts, poor quality and overpriced public works construction, and uncooperative utilities. Reformers could choose their special area of reform. John MacVicar, streets commissioner (later his son held the same position), took on the privately owned utilities. Local ministers worked to eliminate notorious areas of vice and crime. Businessmen, especially members of the Commercial Club (forerunner of the Chamber of Commerce), led in the change to the commission form of government. The Des Moines Women's Club helped develop the downtown riverfront into the present Civic Center district of public buildings.

The 1910s were a decade of enthusiasm and excitement in Polk County.

Vehicles line Fifth Street north through the old ball diamond and circus field in Des Moines. This photograph from 1915 reflects the enthusiasm with which the automobile was received. Courtesy, Des Moines Pioneer Club

The Court Avenue Bridge is seen here in an image from 1910, seven years before the bridge was replaced. The east bank of the Des Moines River was an ugly assemblage of wood pilings, brazen billboards, and refuse. Des Moines residents, in particular the Des Moines Women's Club, remedied this situation through good planning. The result was an attractive and improved riverfront lined with public buildings. Courtesy, Des Moines Pioneer Club

Fueled by the healthy farm market, prosperity was the watchword for many central Iowa households. But beginning in 1915, hostilities in distant Europe filled the front pages of local newspapers. World War I also curtailed European food production, and Iowa farmers stepped in to fill the demand.

It was a time of contrasts in the county, when reforms such as providing settlement houses for the poor competed for news space with Ku Klux Klan meetings and other forms of intolerance. In 1918, during the height of anti-foreign feelings (especially against Germans) surrounding World War I, Iowa's governor William L. Harding banned the use of all languages other than English. The ban even extended to telephone conversations and church services.

The faraway fighting of the First World War also affected Polk County directly. Beginning in 1917, new conscripts streamed into Camp Dodge in Johnston, a National Guard camp which became one of 16 national Army cantonments. The Weitz Company supervised other local contractors during construction of the nearly 2,000 structures at Camp Dodge. It was a logistical nightmare to care for the more than 1,000 teams of horses and mules needed to carry supplies and excavate dirt. Construction costs totaled $12 million and proceeded at such a rapid rate that Camp Dodge was ready to accept draftees in the fall of 1917.

Peace came to the European battlefields on November 11, 1918, too soon for Camp Dodge to develop its full cantonment strength. However, another Des Moines military facility did achieve its mission. Established in 1903 as a cavalry post, the third Fort Des Moines was the first training camp in the nation for black officers. Over the summer of 1917, the Provisional Army Officer Training School trained 1,200 men to lead black infantry and cavalry units. Segregated units were the norm during this period. The 639 graduates commanded black units that received many citations for bravery. The French awarded the coveted Croix de Guerre to the entire First Battalion of the 367th Infantry for its distinguished service.

Facing page, top: Built in 1909-1910, Des Moines' Municipal Building was specifically designed to accommodate the new, more open and responsive style of government under the Des Moines Plan. The massive Counting Room, shown here shortly after construction, housed most government departments in one open room. Note the spittoons carefully arrayed along the patterned marble floor. Courtesy, State Historical Society of Iowa

John MacVicar, Sr. served four terms as mayor of Des Moines and held other elected posts between 1888 and his death in 1928. A leader in progressive governmental reform, he was twice elected president of the League of American Municipalities, an influential urban reform organization. His son, also named John, followed his father into municipal poilitics; the MacVicar Freeway is named to honor their contribution to Des Moines. Courtesy, State Historical Society of Iowa

POLK COUNTY

In 1917 the instant community of Camp Dodge in Johnston provided a variety of services for World War I inductees. Organizations such as the YMCA, Knights of Columbus, and American Library Association built centers for wholesome recreation. Time was filled with compulsory competitive games, drills, and lectures, including French classes for the European-bound soldiers. Courtesy, Des Moines Pioneer Club

The November 14, 1918 parade in Des Moines celebrating the Armistice for World War I lasted over two hours. Military divisions from Camp Dodge and Fort Des Moines No. 3, including four military bands and mounted military police, marched from the Capitol, across the river, and along downtown streets. Civilian groups also got into the act. Uniformed units of high school cadets, fraternal groups, even mail carriers, all joined in the parade. Courtesy, State Historical Society of Iowa

CHANGES WITH THE NEW CENTURY

The world war ended in 1918, and Polk County residents turned to peacetime activities. On July 2, 1919, the Iowa legislature ratified the 19th Amendment to the U.S. Constitution, which allowed women to vote. The following year the Des Moines Chamber of Commerce established a Department of Women's Affairs, reportedly the first of its kind in the country. Another 1919 amendment to the Constitution brought further change to Polk County. The 18th Amendment made the production or sale of alcoholic beverages illegal across the country. America went dry, at least in public.

Events of far more import—those that hit the pocketbook—afflicted many Polk County residents in the 1920s. Despite a national era of prosperity, dramatic changes in the agricultural economy devastated Iowa farmers. With the end of wartime demands for food and fiber, farmers who had increased production and gone into debt by doing so suddenly found themselves with excess farm products. In the summer of 1920 the bottom fell out of the market. By June 1921 hog and cattle prices had fallen by 40 to 50 percent while costs (machinery, taxes, land) remained fixed.

The farm depression rippled through urban economies. The Des Moines Chamber of Commerce—traditionally the most upbeat of groups—characterized 1921 as a period of "the greatest industrial depression and business stagnation" ever. Their employment bureau received 63,000 applications for jobs, but only 13,169 openings were listed.

Despite the economic turmoil and social changes, Des Moines was not completely bereft of improvements in the 1920s. Work on the United States courthouse on the east bank of the riverfront began, and the city's first airport was dedicated. The state's tallest building of the time, the Equitable Life Insurance Company of Iowa office building at 604 Locust, was built in 1923.

The financial difficulties that plagued many central Iowans went national in 1929 with the stock market crash, bank failures, and the related effects on the economy. In 1930 the Des Moines Chamber of Commerce worked for passage of an ordinance to keep all the beggars off the streets of Des Moines, something that had not before been a problem.

New construction did not cease completely, but most major projects were publicly financed. In 1930 Des Moines residents celebrated completion of the first all-paved highway to pass through the Capital City. And in 1932 the Veterans Hospital opened, its oak-filled grounds a charming retreat. Beginning in 1933 large-scale federal relief programs brought public works projects and, more importantly, employment to Polk County. Under the various programs, residents cataloged government documents, painted landscapes (including murals still visible in the women's restroom of the Municipal Building), and sewed garments. Central Fire Station, the river walls and interceptor sewers along the Des Moines

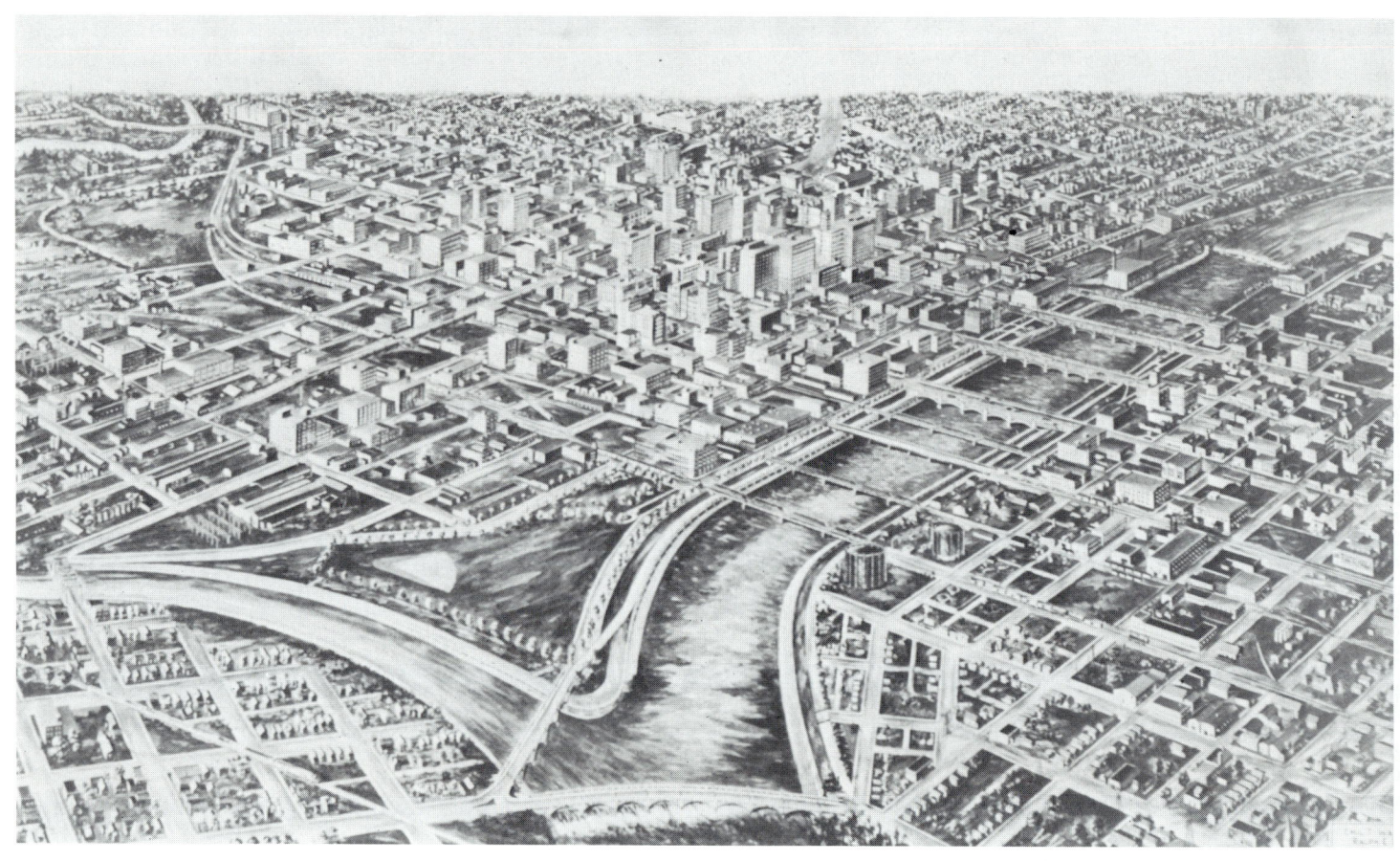

Depression-era work projects included reviving the nineteenth century tradition of the birdseye-view panorama. Artists Emil T. Warns, Frank J. Eisman, and architect Ralph E. Sawyer were responsible for this view. It highlights the riverfront improvements such as new river walls and the Armory, all part of the riverfront Civic Center of public buildings between the Center Street dam and the confluence of the Des Moines and Raccoon rivers. Courtesy, State Historical Society of Iowa

River, and the Argonne Armory were all government projects from the Depression.

The massive federal programs provided employment for many in Polk County. The economy was said to be improving, but again international events intruded and changed the American way of life. On December 7, 1941, Japan attacked Pearl Harbor in Hawaii, decimating the United States' Pacific fleet. The attack launched America into the war against Germany and Japan.

American government and industry mobilized to meet the unprecedented demand for goods. The Depression, soup lines, and massive unemployment were forgotten as America went to war.

A whole new set of restrictions, circumstances, and adjustments defined the role of a generation. The Office of Price Administration controlled and rationed such everyday items as gasoline, sugar, and shoes. Those on the home front planted victory gardens, saved paper, and melted scrap iron and tin. Young men and women hurriedly married. Women went to work in defense plants, replacing men who became soldiers overnight.

In Polk County Fort Des Moines No. 3 continued to be the site for precedent-shattering events. Beginning on July 20, 1942, Fort Des Moines became the site of the nation's first Women's Auxiliary Army Corps (WAAC) training center.

CHANGES WITH THE NEW CENTURY

Federal Works Progress Administration (WPA) programs during the Great Depression encompassed more than the construction projects which employed men for manual labor. Pictured here on January 31, 1940, is a WPA sewing room in Des Moines where 400 women toiled over sewing machines in two shifts. Garments they fashioned were distributed to the needy in Iowa. Courtesy, State Historical Society of Iowa

The present river walls along the Des Moines River in downtown Des Moines came about as a result of government projects designed to provide employment during the 1930s Depression. The system channels storm run-off from Bird's Run, a stream that roughly follows present Keosauqua Way. Courtesy, Barbara Beving Long

Sergeants Robert W. Thornton and Earl F. Peters, Des Moines natives, were both with the Second Marine regiment in the Pacific. Shown here in the fall of 1944, they saw action at Tarawa, Saipan, and Tinian. Courtesy, State Historical Society of Iowa

Training began with 440 officer candidates and 330 enlisted women, but the numbers grew rapidly, surpassing 70,000 by war's end. The fort lacked sufficient housing for these growing enlistments, and the army simply took over Des Moines hotels. The Savery, Plaza, and Chamberlain hotels, the Oransky Building, the Coliseum, and three Drake University buildings all became barracks for the Second Regiment. For the first time the streets of Des Moines were filled with women in uniform.

World War II also prompted the establishment of related industry. Between 1942 and 1945, the United States Rubber Company operated the Des Moines Ordnance Plant, the largest wartime industry in the area. Located just south of Ankeny, the cartridge-making plant opened in January 1942, just seven months after the 4,442-acre site had been farmland. At its peak it employed 19,000 people.

Polk County residents followed news of each campaign with an interest often heavily tinged with personal emotions. They read about North Africa, the assault on Italy, then D-Day on June 6, 1944, when the Allies invaded France from the sea. Attention turned to the Pacific, culminating on August 6, 1945, when America dropped an atomic bomb on the Japanese city of Hiroshima. A month later Japan surrendered.

Iowans born in the 1880s had endured, and sometimes enjoyed, a host of inconceivable changes at virtually all levels of their lives by the end of the 1940s. Some had traveled the ocean, then across half the continent to reach central Iowa. All had ridden on trains, horse-drawn wagons, then interurbans and automobiles. Half had started their adult life barred from voting. Polk County residents had ridden to new heights of economic prosperity, then seen the depths of a protracted financial depression. They participated in not one, but two world wars.

In the midst of all this overwhelming change, certain sectors remained constant, forming a foundation for weathering economic and social disruption. Iowans' commitment to home, family, church, and school provided a bulwark against the often incomprehensible changes swirling about them.

CHANGES WITH THE NEW CENTURY

WAACs in uniform, a banner exhorting the patriotic to "buy war bonds," and a newsboy bearing news of a sunken U.S. carrier dominate this image of downtown Des Moines at Sixth and Locust in September 1942. Courtesy, State Historical Society of Iowa

Three of the seven spires of "Piety Hill" make up this view north on Eighth Street around 1915. First Baptist (left) and Central Presbyterian stood safely on either side of Eighth Street. Plymouth Congregational, however, stood in the path of automotive progress and was condemned for road construction in 1925. Courtesy, Des Moines Pioneer Club

CHAPTER SIX

Beyond Subsistence

The earliest white settlers of Polk County concentrated on choosing a farm site and making it habitable. Getting in the crops and building a house were important and basic activities. Town residents—perhaps "town" was an overstatement, given the crude living conditions—went about opening general stores, land offices, and law offices. Despite the subsistence level of living, Polk County residents were quick to establish such fundamental institutions as schools and churches.

The first schools in Fort Des Moines (and the county) dated from 1846, the first year of legal settlement. In that year both Mary Davis and Lewis Whitten offered instruction. Only those parents who were able to pay could send their children to these private schools. The conditions were less than ideal: the students met in the former barracks cabins that had been Fort Des Moines No. 2.

The establishment of schools followed similar patterns throughout the county. From humble beginnings and classes held wherever possible grew a network of country schools. Surprisingly small areas contained a locally controlled, independent school district. An 1875 map shows some 130 town and country schools in Polk County.

The era of the small, independent school districts around Des Moines came to a close with the turn of the century. In 1907 a consolidated district, the Independent Community School District of Des Moines, merged the east and west sides as well as the over 20 suburban districts. By 1910, 17,123 pupils were enrolled, the second-largest total after Utah's Salt Lake City among cities with a population of less than 100,000. Private schools added to the number of students. For example, about 250 girls attended St. Joseph's Academy, founded in 1911.

Establishment of institutions of higher learning also dated from the pioneer settlement era in Polk County. The motivation behind their establishment was generated more by boosterism than by a commitment to academic

Drake University students learn the mysteries of chemistry in Science Hall under the guidance of Professor Charles Noyes Kinney who is seen attending to a student near the blackboard. Daniel W. Morehouse, shown at the lower right, was a student in the late 1890s. An astronomer by training, in 1908 he discovered an unusual comet that bears his name. From 1922 until his death in 1941, Morehouse was President of Drake University. Courtesy, Drake University

excellence. Des Moines' first college was built in 1855 but never opened. In 1864 Des Moines University (later College), a Baptist school, began classes in the building constructed for the 1855 phantom college. The history of the school was marked by continual financial difficulties, slow growth, and competition with another Baptist school, Central College in Pella, just 30 miles away.

Unlike a host of defunct colleges in Iowa, Drake University in Des Moines was eminently successful in creating a solid financial footing. In 1881 the faculty of Disciples of Christ-sponsored Oskaloosa College abandoned the foundering school. They all moved to the newly created Drake University, also a Disciples of Christ school. The Drake campus lay in the new suburb of University Place, just northwest of the Des Moines city limits.

The college was named for its principal backer, General Francis M. Drake, but only after he agreed to donate $20,000. By the time of his death in 1903, the former Iowa governor and Civil War general had donated at least $232,076 to Drake University.

Through judicious sale of residential lots in University Place, Drake University added to its financial reserves and also created a distinct community around its campus in the bargain. It appears that Drake University was the only Iowa college directly involved in real estate platting and selling and (later) apartment construction. Drake University was the fastest-growing college in the state during the late nineteenth century.

Old Main, the first building for Grand View College, was built in three parts. The first section, shown here in 1895, was matched by a second wing, one not connected to it. Then, in 1904, a central part was added which united the two wings. The building is modeled after Belmont Seminary, an 1890 school in Bedford, Virginia. However, Old Main reflects its Danish heritage in the design of the elaborate front dormer. From An Illustrated History of Des Moines, *1895*

Another Des Moines college followed Drake University's lead in offering lots for sale. Between 1889 and 1893 a Des Moines Danish leader, Middel Lauritsen, worked with the Danish-American Church to bring a Lutheran seminary to Des Moines. The church finally agreed, provided the Des Moines backers sold a specified number of lots around the college site north of Union Park and built a foundation for a school building (Old Main) by 1894.

The terms of the agreement were met, but growth was slow. In contrast with Drake University, Grand View College offered a highly specialized curriculum designed to train Danish-speaking students for the Lutheran ministry.

Built in 1910-1912, East High School was the first of the twentieth century high schools to be built in Des Moines. A beacon for east side pride, it is the only Des Moines school faced entirely with limestone. The design is a teaching device for studying ancient architecture. The projecting north entrance and steps shown here are modeled after the Erechtheum in Athens, Greece, a temple dating from 421-405 B.C. Courtesy, State Historical Society of Iowa

Organized in 1857, Plymouth Congregational Church is among the oldest congregations in Des Moines. Sometime before 1865 the original frame church was moved from its Fourth and Court location to Locust Street at Seventh. Pictured at its new site, the church was enlarged and adorned with a blend of Gothic Revival and Romanesque Revival details. Courtesy, Public Library of Des Moines

Above, right: When Thomas Mitchell established a new town by the railroad, he donated a church site and also the bell for the Universalist Church. Photographed shortly after it was built in 1868, it was the first church in Mitchellville. Courtesy, State Historical Society of Iowa

With the relatively small numbers of Danes in Des Moines, the school had to draw on the Danish community from all over the Midwest. But the school has persisted, and in 1975 Grand View College added a full, four-year program to its courses.

Religion played a prominent role in the early history of Polk County, and a number of denominations were represented. However, the Methodist church dominated in the nineteenth century because of the circuit rider system it employed. The Methodists established territories and sent out ministers to visit settlements, no matter how small. These communities or clusters of farms were too small to support a resident minister and church. When there were sufficient numbers to found a church, however, it was as often as not a Methodist one. In Fort Des Moines the first Methodist church was built in 1846.

By 1895 over 14 percent of the 72,888 Polk County residents called themselves Methodists. The next highest group, with 9 percent, belonged to the Christian church. Catholics and Lutherans were evenly represented at 7 percent each. There were goodly representations of Presbyterians (4 percent), Baptists (3 percent), Congregationalists (3 percent), Episcopalians (2 percent), Jews (one percent), and United Brethren (one percent). A sprinkling of Mennonites, Dunkards, Friends, Universalists, and Latter-day Saints, among others, rounded out religious representation.

Church services and related social gatherings provided an important means for socializing on the prairie. Farm life could be quite isolated, and the prospect of meeting and greeting friends must have been a distinct pleasure. Nonreligious celebrations and events were similarly slow-paced and tradition-filled by modern standards. In 1853 Des Moines residents celebrated the Fourth of July with a reading of the Declaration of

Des Moines residents organized the First German Methodist Episcopal Church in 1856. Ten years later, as the sign above the door proclaims, the immigrant congregation built this unassuming church at the corner of Second and Locust streets. The congregation held services there until at least 1894. Courtesy, State Historical Society of Iowa

Independence and an oration by attorney Daniel O. Finch. There was a procession led by the President of the Day, followed by a series of toasts and responses, the benediction, and a public dinner.

Another secular and thoroughly Iowan entertainment was the state fair. After years of discussion, the legislature appropriated $50,000 in 1885 for a permanent state fair site in Des Moines, provided that Des Moines residents raise a like amount. With sufficient funds in hand, the state bought the Calvin Thornton farm three miles east of the state capitol.

The first fair opened at its permanent site on September 3, 1886. The 67 buildings included barns for cattle and horses, exhibition halls, and 50 wells. "The main buildings [were] on the side of a hill thickly wooded with native trees and overlooking the amphitheater and all the stock barns and pens," according to a contemporary newspaper account.

The emphasis of the Iowa State Fair began and remained agricultural. Generations of Iowa youth proudly brought their carefully groomed livestock to the fair for judging. But the fair has also grown and evolved over its more than 100-year history. Local television stations move to the fairgrounds every August. Fairgoers consume corndogs, Iowa chops, cotton candy, and ice cream. They visit the Varied Industries Building and pick up a free hat or bag. They tour the sheep, hog, cattle, poultry, and horse barns where exhibitors sleep on cots near their animals. They inspect the huge tomatoes on display in the Horticulture Building, never failing to pass by the butter cow. They wander through the midway, listening to the hawkers of games nearly impossible to win. They enjoy a show in the grandstand and marvel at the nightly fireworks display.

The Iowa State Fair has been a fixture in Des Moines for over 100 years.

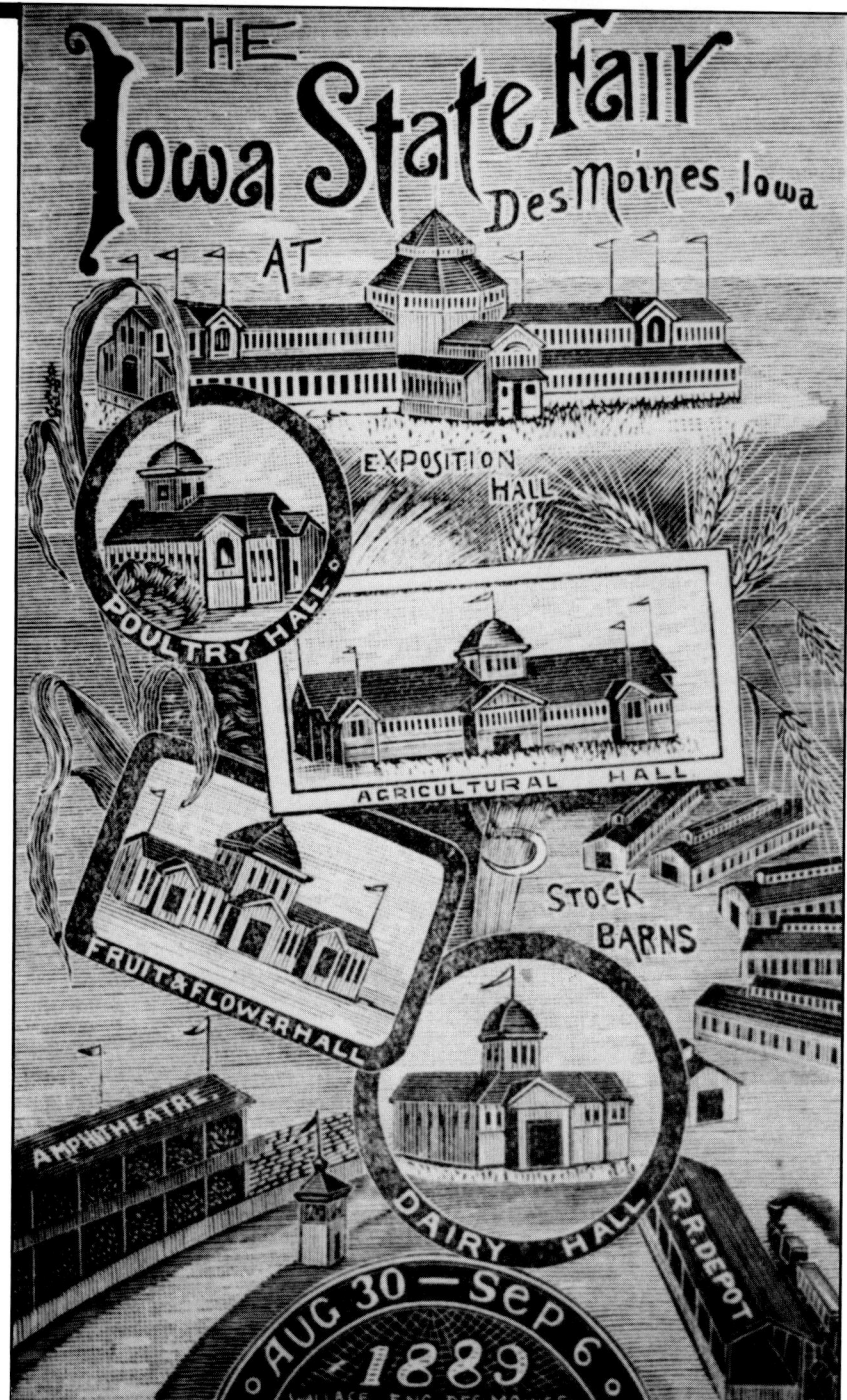

This advertisement for the 1889 State Fair spotlighted the exhibition halls and other facilities that contributed to the fair's overwhelming success in its first four years of existence. Courtesy, State Historical Society of Iowa

Other forms of local entertainment have nearly as venerable a standing. The festival known as Seni-Om-Sed (Des Moines spelled backwards) dates from the early 1880s. Since the state fair was then open only during the day, Des Moines boosters organized Seni-Om-Sed to provide night entertainment during fair time. By the 1890s the event had become quite elaborate. There were open-air band concerts, free circus and midway shows, and a floral parade featuring floats with such themes as the "Boston Tea Party" or "General Lee's Surrender". The streets were brightly lit, and Japanese fireworks and a "Battle of Manila" pyrotechnic display illuminated the skies over the Des Moines River in 1898. For the 1897 festival President William McKinley opened festivities by touching an electric button in Washington, D.C., that exploded "the signal bomb in the magnificent river spectacle, the Running of the Batteries of Vicksburg."

Amusement parks, often at the end of a streetcar line, also dated from the 1880s in Des Moines. In fact, streetcar mogul Jefferson Polk established both Crocker Woods and Ingersoll Park as destinations for Sunday passengers on his streetcar lines. Crocker Park predated the Zoological Gardens, Union Park, and Riverview Park as a recreation spot on the Des Moines River north of downtown. People could also take the ferry or their own boats to these riverfront parks.

Ingersoll Park was located in the 4,000 blocks between Grand and Ingersoll avenues. The amusement park featured elephants and other exotic animals, a roller coaster, and a bandstand. When there was sufficient demand for new housing around 1913, the owners closed the park and platted homesites. Acres of fine homes now occupy the old amusement park.

Located on the site of the former Zoological Gardens off Sixth Avenue in 1915, Riverview Park had rides, a fine

Proud pig raisers of all ages display what they hope will be prize-winning animals at the Fair. Livestock, the latest in farming technology, and the butter cow are just some of the attractions that have made the Fair a regular success. Courtesy, State Historical Society of Iowa

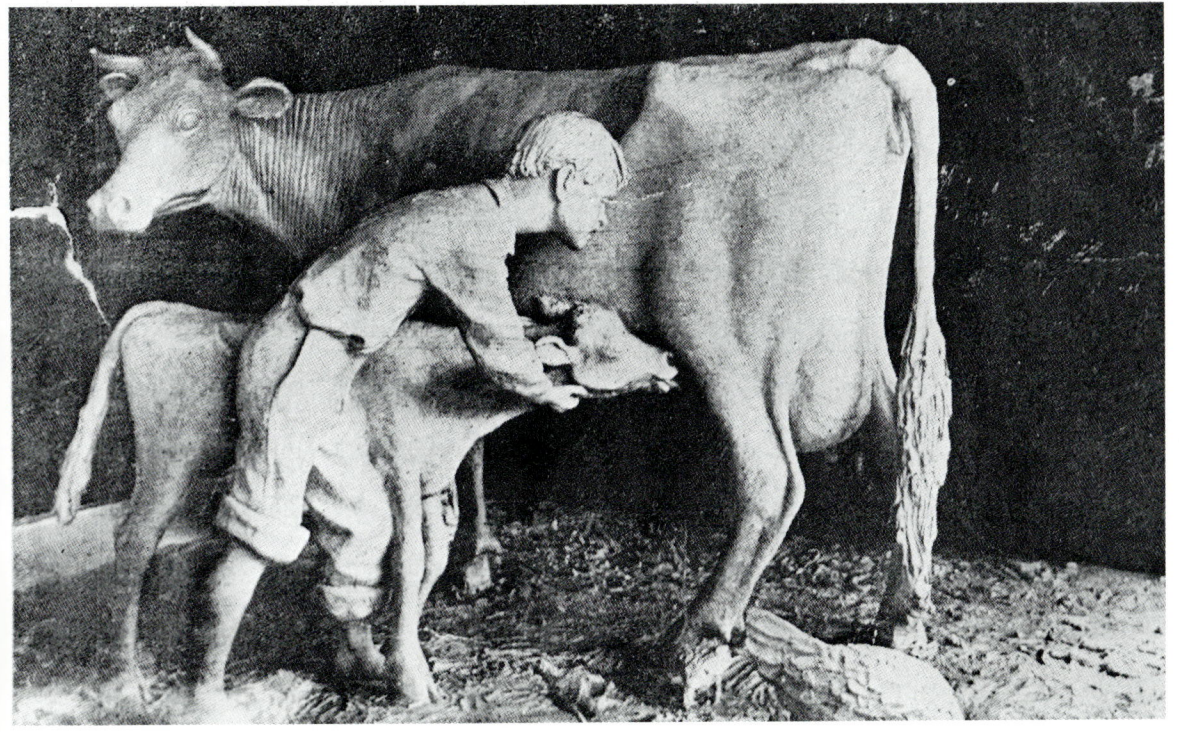

While Iowa has traditionally led the nation in corn and hog production, dairying has also played an important role in the agricultural economy. In 1899 Iowa was ranked as the greatest butter-producing state in the nation. All but two counties had creameries, which produced 88,000,000 pounds of butter a year. Nowhere was the strength of the dairy industry in Iowa better reflected than at the State Fair butter cow exhibition. Courtesy, State Historical Society of Iowa

merry-go-round, the Ghost House, and the Mirror Maze. In the early days, admission was a nickel for those on foot, and a dime to drive over the bridge that crossed the lagoon. (The lagoon was really an old sand pit, but such was the magic that Riverview conjured up.)

Riverview lives on, in part, at Adventureland in Altoona, Iowa's first theme park. The owners of Adventureland bought out Riverview, closed it in 1979, and re-created the flavor of Riverview in a corner of the park. Spread over 200 acres, Adventureland, with its wonderful roller coaster, imaginary Main Street, and many rides, is not on the riverfront nor is it at the end of a streetcar line. It is on the modern transportation counterpart of the streetcar line: an interstate highway. A horse racing track is under construction near it, offering entertainment of another sort.

POLK COUNTY

The twentieth century brought new types of entertainment to Polk County: vaudeville and the motion picture. The 1910s saw a revolution in viewing tastes. Opera houses closed or were converted to vaudeville and movie houses.

These arching light displays at Fourth and Walnut streets were just some of the arrangements made for the Seni-Om-Sed celebration in 1897. Among the attractions during the 1897 festivities was "world-famed Ida Fuller" executing "her marvelous fire dances on an immense barge in the river." Some of the spirit of the original Seni-Om-Sed festival was revived in 1982 as a weekly summertime event in downtown Des Moines. Courtesy, State Historical Society of Iowa

One of the benefits of serving on the school safety patrol was an annual picnic at Riverview Park. In recognition for seeing their schoolmates safely across street intersections, hundreds of children received free admission to Des Moines' favorite amusement park every June. Courtesy, State Historical Society of Iowa

The Grand Opera House on Fourth between Walnut and Locust was among those to meet that fate. It was rechristened the Berchel and turned into a motion picture palace. Live theater did not disappear, however. Just across the street was the white terra cotta Princess Theater. Beginning in 1909, Kip Elbert and Jack Getchell managed the Princess Theater's stock company. For 19 years they put on a new play every week of the 40-week season.

Elbert and Getchell also opened the first movie house in Iowa, the Nickeldom, in 1905. By 1916 there were 28 theaters dotting downtown Des Moines. Going to the movies became a Saturday night ritual. Patrons watched the latest episode in such serials as *The Perils of Pauline* and *The Million Dollar Mystery.*

Many of the forms of entertainment that charmed Des Moines and Polk County residents could also be found throughout the country. Traveling stock companies, vaudeville revues, lecturers, and movies came to many cities and towns across America. But only in Des Moines was the "Des Moines City Waltz" a hit. Will Lehman, local musician and music store owner, penned the work and copyrighted it sometime between 1864 and 1870.

The work was rediscovered when local architect William J. Wagner found the sheet music in a Kansas City used bookstore. The Des Moines Municipal Band played the piece at a 1961 "Music Under the Stars" concert on the capitol grounds. Other musical works are named for the capital city: two named "Des Moines," two "Des Moines Songs," the "Des Moines Blues," "Des Moines, Yes Ma'am," and the "Greater Des Moines March."

Des Moines is also the subject of many paintings. Des Moines businessman James S. Carpenter was among those who fostered the arts in Des Moines. He helped found the Des Moines Association of Fine Arts in 1916, forerunner of the present Art Center. As an arts patron he opened his home to painters. His house still stands on East 33rd Street not far from the fairgrounds; it has a special room-sized vault for artwork. Gardner Symons, an artist known for his winter scenes, painted scenes of Four Mile Creek during his stay with Carpenter.

The name Charles Atherton Cumming was synonymous with art in Des Moines. In 1895 the artist founded the Cumming School of Art. He later taught at the University of Iowa and also at Cornell College in Mount Vernon, Iowa. Until 1928 the school was housed on the third floor of the Public Library of Des Moines. No less than 19 portraits by Cumming made their way into the collection of the State Historical Society of Iowa, and his mural, *The Departure of the Indian from Iowa*, adorns the Polk County Courthouse.

Des Moines has also been immortalized through the printed word. *Murder in the Library*, a 1930s mystery, is dedicated to then-director of the Public Library of Des Moines, Forrest Spaulding,

In 1878 Charles G. Lewis opened the Lewis Opera Hall in the three-story building that still stands near East Sixth on East Locust Street. The ornate interior, shown here in the 1880s, featured crimson and gold leaf borders and elegant metal Corinthian columns. There were marble busts of George Washington and Abraham Lincoln above the two private boxes, and a dome with a gas chandelier. The drop curtain shown here featured an Italian harbor scene. Courtesy, Des Moines Pioneer Club

and his staff. The setting and details do not really conform to Des Moines, but the author, Rev. Charles J. Dutton, used his familiarity with the library in Des Moines as the basis for the mystery. Dutton, who had been a lawyer and journalist, was pastor of the First Unitarian Church in Des Moines for about 10 years in the 1920s.

Writing in 1933, Des Moines native Ruth Stewart, a journalist and Hollywood writer, was much more faithful to Des Moines, its setting, and residents in Capital City. Stewart's city is called Les Quats, also a mangled French name. One of the main characters is James B. Gaskett, newly elected governor. Like Clyde Herring, who was elected Iowa's governor in 1932, the fictional Gaskett was the first Democrat elected to that post in decades.

In the course of following the exploits of a woman reporter, a dashing foreigner, and the kidnapping of the governor, the book describes Grand Avenue and its change from a quiet residential thoroughfare: "They passed the Ford factory [later Tech High School], the rival undertakers, the ornate mansions converted into fraternal homes or insurance offices, and slowed down in front of the crenelated tower [Terrace Hill] of the lone millionaire."

Des Moines and Polk County are also the fictionalized setting for Tom Duncan's *Gus the Great*. The novel sold 750,000 copies in the 1940s. In it the author, a native of Iowa, mentions Des

The excitement and pageantry of the Iowa State Fair were captured in these colorful posters during the late 1800s and early 1900s. Courtesy, State Historical Society of Iowa

Above: Work on the capitol interior began in the 1880s and continued through the early 1900s. Attention to detail and ornate decoration characterize the building and add to its splendor. Photo by Bill Nellans

Right: Built on the same hillside as the first capitol building, today's capitol commands a sweeping view of the Des Moines and Raccoon rivers. Photo by Dana Downie

Facing page, top: The capitol building, the railroad, farming, and agriculture are all elegantly represented in this stained glass window from the Teachout Building in Des Moines. Courtesy, East Des Moines Club

Facing page, bottom left: This statue welcomes visitors to the capitol building in Des Moines. Photo by Bill Nellans

Facing page, bottom right: Des Moines remains one of the most liveable cities in the nation. Steady growth and its position as a leading insurance center are but some of the factors that have contributed to the city's eminence. Photo by Bill Nellans

Above: Rural and big city life exist hand-in-hand in Polk County and are part of what makes the region unique. Photo by Bill Nellans

Right: The Bondurant Coop, like other cooperatives, serves as a springboard for local farmers eager to market their goods. Photo by Michael E. Petersen

Big Creek State Park outside Polk City offers visitors recreation in the form of hiking, fishing, and boating. Photo by Michael E. Petersen

Facing page, top: Local waters, including Des Moines' twin rivers and Red Rock and Saylorville lakes, are ideal for fishing and boating. Photo by Bill Nellans

Facing page, bottom: The Civic Center in downtown Des Moines offers entertainment ranging from classical music to more contemporary rock shows. Photo by Bill Nellans

Above: The geodesic Botanical Center in Des Moines houses a diverse and interesting group of plants from around the world. The center is a welcome addition to a city with roots in agriculture. Photo by Bill Nellans

Left: The Sculpture "Chauchuc Grid" by artist Scopia of St. Louis graces the entrance to the new Regency West 4 office building. Courtesy, Mid-America Group Ltd.

96

Right: Living History Farms transports visitors to the past to experience a way of life that existed over 100 years ago. Courtesy, Miriam Dunlap

Below: The immense Salisbury House on Des Moines' Tonawanda Drive was modeled after King's House in Salisbury, England. Built in 1928 by cosmetics manufacturer Carl Weeks, it houses a major collection of ancient furniture, paintings, and art objects. Photo by Bill Nellans

Moines ("Tamarack"), West Des Moines ("Clayton Junction"), and painter Grant Wood ("Alex Kerry"). The principal setting and characters are based on William and Fred Buchanan's circus, the Yankee Robinson Shows. The Buchanan circus wintered on a farm in Polk County near Granger. Before going on the road each spring, Buchanan would put on a circus parade. The circus folded its tent in 1930.

Polk County residents established and enjoyed a variety of institutions. Some were fundamental parts of society, such as churches and schools, while others provided recreational or artistic diversions. Several of them—the Iowa State Fair, movies, the many religious denominations, and a large school system—have remained to enrich and improve lives. Succeeding decades have brought further change, not always for the better, but the continuum of questioning, revision, and action has persisted.

This display tent on East Fifth and Locust reflected the importance of agriculture in Polk County. The display was part of an annual corn show sponsored by merchants from the east side of Des Moines. Held through the 1910s, the show was designed to lure shoppers to the east side and to promote Iowa agriculture. Courtesy, Des Moines Pioneer Club

John Ruan has been one of the most influential men in Iowa. A self-made millionaire, he began his career in 1933 at the age of 19. With a single truck he began hauling gravel in Mahaska County. He soon switched to hauling gasoline and thus had one of the state's earliest trucking operations specializing in gasoline. The truck shown here is part of the 1946 Iowa Centennial parade held in Des Moines. Courtesy, State Historical Society of Iowa

CHAPTER SEVEN

Heritage of Achievement

During a visit in 1941, city planning consultant Harland Bartholomew commented that Des Moines citizens lacked the spirit and pride to improve their city. In a stunning turnaround from previous decades when optimism and action were the watchwords among Des Moines leaders, Bartholomew concluded: "There seems to be nobody interested in making it a good city and in preserving values. There is less public spirit here than in almost any city I have ever been in."

Bartholomew was in a good position to evaluate this seeming change. His St. Louis consulting firm had begun preparing city plans for Des Moines in the 1920s, returning every 10 years or so to revise them. In his 1941 remarks Bartholomew may have been delivering deliberately inflammatory pronouncements in the hopes of rekindling the sparks of community spirit.

Statements about community spirit aside, factors beyond the control of Des Moines residents worked to hinder a healthy and growing downtown Des Moines. The major role of federal money in backing local improvements and construction projects began during the Depression and continued during the years after World War II. Using federal money, Des Moines had built bridges, river walls, new streets, and an addition to the post office, among other projects in the 1930s.

In the postwar decades federal money continued to flow into central Iowa, but not always to Des Moines. Downtown Des Moines, its riverfront, street systems, and federal buildings were no longer the sole, or even primary, recipients of federal largess. In 1958 Congress authorized Saylorville Dam in Polk County on the Des Moines River north of the Capital City. Two years later both the Saylorville and Red Rock dams (just south of the county) were funded. Construction soon began on these projects, bringing fine recreational facilities as well as flood control measures to the north and south of Des Moines.

Walnut Street near Seventh has long been the heart of retail shopping in Des Moines. In 1940 no less than 10 women's shops, including a furrier and two shoe stores, lined Walnut between Seventh and Eighth streets. The Utica Clothing Store, F.W. Woolworth Company, and S.S. Kresge Company, seen here on the north side of Walnut between Sixth and Seventh streets, also catered to shoppers. Courtesy, State Historical Society of Iowa

Also in the late 1950s and early 1960s, a new transportation system injected a profound and far-reaching change in Polk County. Just as construction of railroad lines had prompted settlement of such rail stops as Clive, Ankeny, and Runnells in the nineteenth century, the interstate highway system directly influenced development along its routes beginning in the 1960s. Two systems, the east-west Interstate 80 and the north-south Interstate 35, intersect just west of Des Moines near Clive, Urbandale, and West Des Moines. They link Polk County with the 41,000-mile interstate system that crisscrosses the country.

In 1958 federal, state, and local officials announced final plans for construction of a 13.5-mile freeway through Des Moines to connect the city with the western suburbs and the interstates. Taken by the highway monolith were more than 1,000 dwellings, some 50 businesses, 3 churches, and a like number of schools.

New construction—thousands of houses, shopping malls, strips of retail shops, and fast food eateries—replaced them. Thoroughly modern office buildings, with gleaming windows and hard edges, went up on landscaped suburban sites along the freeway. The new buildings and malls look like freeway-related construction throughout the nation; a leveling of appearance has been the price of change. In all of metropolitan Des Moines, construction of commercial space amounted to more than $1 billion and added 7.4 million square feet of space between 1980 and 1987, much of it along the freeway.

With easy access assured, Des Moines residents expressed their preference for westward residential expansion. The suburbs of West Des Moines, Urbandale, Windsor Heights, Clive, and Johnston grew overnight into expanses of tract housing on former rolling farmland. The 1880s rail stop of Clive, not even incorporated until 1956, mush-

HERITAGE OF ACHIEVEMENT

roomed from 752 people to 2,948 between 1960 and 1970, and reached 5,906 in 1980. West Des Moines, the former railroad town of Valley Junction, hosted the most growth. Building permits were issued there for 2,391 housing units between 1980 and 1985.

Forces beyond the corporate limits of Des Moines, much of them federally sponsored, were at work to sap urban vitality. But downtown leaders may also have felt a certain complacency in the postwar years. They seemed at a loss to compete with the allure of shopping malls and other suburban construction. The complacency or lack of spirit that Bartholomew detected in 1941 eventually gave way to dissatisfaction and a certain amount of foundering as residents tried to grapple with the alleged death of the "Loop," as downtown Des Moines was, and still is, known.

The urban center of Des Moines did receive federal monies, but the program was a negative approach to development, calling for the leveling of at least 300 acres of land, most just north of downtown, and displacing hundreds of households. The project moved slowly; it took time to buy and bulldoze homes. Many were irreplaceable Victorian houses, but this was before the current interest in living in such fine old neighborhoods as Sherman Hill. In 1957 the Iowa legislature voted to authorize urban renewal projects, and the following year the federal government approved the project. In 1962 the first parcel of federally razed land was sold to a private developer.

Redevelopment of the steep, inner-city section north of downtown continued gradually. New federal projects aimed at providing low-income housing (especially for those displaced through the previous federal urban renewal program) were built in the area. In 1968, the Model Cities program began. Many small office buildings now extend along Sixth and Second avenues to the freeway.

Beginning in the early 1960s downtown Des Moines leaders began to act, in an effort to move from the stage of dissatisfaction and questioning, into the direction of concrete change. The end result was by no means assured. Many still felt that the downtown was forever dead and could never be resuscitated.

In 1984 the population of Ankeny reached 16,442. In 1941, however, it remained a small and peaceful town. Despite Ankeny's modest size, basic services such as a bank, bakery and grocery, restaurant, variety store, and drug store were all represented. Courtesy, State Historical Society of Iowa

The curving steel and concrete elevated highways of the interstate system have a stark modern beauty. The overpass shown in this 1967 photograph is located on Interstate-80 near the Second Avenue exit. Courtesy, State Historical Society of Iowa

When the Merle Hay Plaza Shopping Center opened in 1959, its six buildings transformed the formerly rural location of Douglas Avenue and Merle Hay Road. The new retail center, the largest in Iowa, covered 665,000 square feet and housed 30 shops, as well as the department stores of Younkers and Sears. Shoppers flocked to the shopping center, availing themselves of the more than 4,000 free parking spaces and a 36-lane subterranean bowling alley. Courtesy, State Historical Society of Iowa

But there was reason for cautious optimism. The economic base of the city was sound. Industrial employment had grown; the agricultural implement giant, Massey-Ferguson, moved its North American headquarters to Des Moines in 1965. A national retail chain, J.C. Penney, decided to lease a new downtown store, rather than flee to the suburban malls. In 1961 a new $10-million federal office building at Second and Walnut received federal approval. Financial institutions put up new buildings, including the 16-story Central National Bank & Trust Company building at Sixth and Locust, and the Home Federal Savings & Loan building. Internationally acclaimed architect Mies van der Rohe designed the latter building at Sixth and Grand. American Republic Insurance constructed a suitably modern office building at Sixth and Keo, on the site of the Victoria Hotel. Its sculpture court housed a modern abstract metal sculpture, proof positive that Des Moines was alive and kicking.

On the other side of the 1960s balance sheet, major retailers such as Ward's and Sears closed their downtown stores and moved to the malls. Deteriorating vacant buildings such as Davidson's department store on Walnut could be found on far too many blocks. Many small, locally owned shops closed. Once-proud Court Avenue, the mid-nineteenth century commercial hub of the city, had drifted into disrepute. Its Victorian wholesale buildings housed peep shows, cheap boardinghouses, and bars.

The winds of change and hope were in the air in the 1960s, but 1972 was the bellwether year for change and marked the beginning of the long-sought renaissance of downtown Des Moines. Announced in that year were plans to construct the 25-story Financial Center and the 36-story Ruan Center. The Civic Center, Botanical Center, and most recently the Convention Center have emerged from plans first announced in 1972.

Fund-raising for Nollen Plaza and the nearly 3,000-seat Civic Center—an urgently needed replacement for KRNT Theatre which closed in 1972—became the largest private construction effort ever in the city. Residents and corporations contributed over $9.3 million.

Suddenly it seemed okay to be downtown. In 1977 another public institution, the Des Moines Area Community College, announced it would locate an urban campus on the near north side. Another publicly funded project was the Walnut Street Transit Mall. Extending from Second to Tenth, the attractive mall features covered waiting areas for Metro Transit riders and lanes for buses only. Beginning in 1985 the new Convention Center provided meeting space to supplement Veterans Memorial Auditorium. On the city's east side, the principal public construction was the State of

The KRNT Theater was built in 1925 by the Za-Ga-Zig Shrine Temple at a cost of $1 million. In 1957 the 3,600-seat facility was filled to capacity for the Metropolitan Opera. It was the traveling Grand Ole Opry, however, that consistently packed them in until a leaky roof forced closing of the theater in 1972. Courtesy, State Historical Society of Iowa

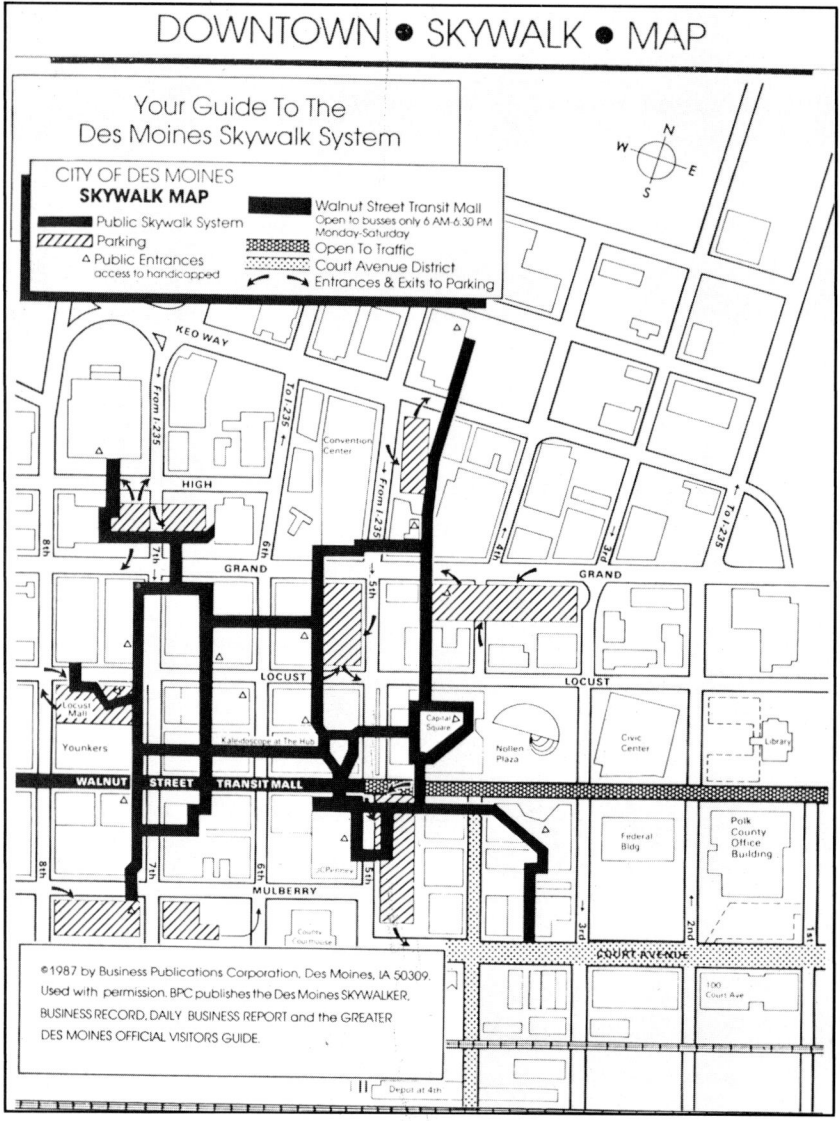

The 1988 version of the 31-bridge skywalk system in Des Moines attracts conventioneers to the night life of Court Avenue from their hotels and the Convention Center. Shoppers and elderly residents also benefit from the system by using it to reach department stores and shops or for recreational strolling. © Business Publications Corporation, Des Moines, IA

Iowa Historical Building which opened in 1987. There were ever more parking garages, totaling seven that same year. It was a wonderful time to be involved in construction work.

A new concept, "planned, climate-controlled access" to buildings, physically united many of these new projects, and symbolized the spirit of public and private cooperation evident in the 1970s and 1980s. The first skywalk, as it was soon christened, opened in 1971 and linked the new J.C. Penney store with a parking garage. In 1975 Mayor Richard Olson announced the federal government would pay most of the costs for skywalks that would initially connect a 12-block area. Des Moines was on its way to becoming a "weatherproof city." Shoppers, workers, and conventioneers alike no longer needed to brave the elements to move from place to place. By 1988 31 skywalks crossed Des Moines' streets and connected more than 30 buildings over 21 blocks.

Convenience has not come without paying the price, however. Skywalks now mask the once-majestic view of the state capitol from Locust Street. And these elevated passages are awkwardly affixed to buildings at some points.

A crucial ingredient to the success of these and related projects was the partnership forged between the private and public sectors. Not without controversy, the city gave attractive financial incentives for new construction downtown. An active and respected city manager, Richard Wilkey, worked well with Mayor Richard Olson, elected in 1972. Olson was responsible in large part for sparking the change, and a plaque on the skywalks commends "his vision and foresight."

Businessman John Ruan emerged as one of the most influential leaders behind the 1970s resurgence of downtown Des Moines. Through his efforts and the work of Wilkey, Olson, real estate developer William Knapp, Hubbell family interests, and members of the Greater Des Moines Committee (and later, the Downtown Development Corporation), retail, office, residential, and cultural buildings alike have gone up. In the 10 years between 1971 and 1981, more then $313 million was spent on redeveloping downtown Des Moines.

Success bred success, resulting in over a dozen major new buildings downtown. By 1980 the following projects were nearly ready for occupants: the 30-story Marriott Hotel, Locust Street Mall, Carriers Insurance office building, and the atrium-style offices and shops in Capital Square. Also opening in the 1980s were the elaborate Kaleidoscope group of shops and the related Hub office building, and a costly office building for the Principal Financial Group (formerly Bankers Life Insurance). Des Moines had the makings of a skyline.

Not only were there new places to work and shop, there were new places to live in downtown Des Moines. The small-scale Civic Center Court on the old City Market site at Second and Locust was the first new residential housing built downtown. First Baptist Church led in the 1980s with construction of two major projects providing housing for the elderly: the 17-story Elsie Mason Manor and the 13-story Ligutti Tower. St. John's Lutheran Church also sponsored a multi-story housing complex. Plaza condominiums at Third and Walnut, also a 1980s project, soon followed, providing high-rise living for those of any age.

Redevelopment spread to the commercial sector east of the river, bringing the two competing sides of town closer together. The near east side is for the first time considered part of downtown Des Moines. The Hubbell family interests built a series of low, red brick offices called Capitol Center along East Walnut. The Principal Financial Group sponsored another group of low-rise offices at East First and Locust. Hawkeye Capital Bank replaced the venerable, dark-red brick Capital City Bank Building at East 5th and Locust with its new building, also of dark-red brick.

Des Moines belatedly joined the ranks of historic preservationists when residents began to appreciate the sterling qualities of some old buildings —and the substantial tax breaks possible for approved changes. Renovations have occurred on both sides of the river and include the Northwestern Hotel on the east side and the present Valley National Bank Building, Hotel Fort Des Moines, and the Homestead Building on the west side. "Urban pioneers" have moved to Sherman Hill and reclaimed the many old mansions for their homes. An interest in preserving and appreciating old buildings has prompted the redevelopment of Court Avenue. The Saddlery Building, the Kurtz Warehouse, and the Hawkeye Insurance Company building all host uses far different from their original ones. Even the Court Avenue bridge was reconstructed carefully to save the original elaborate detail. The city spent $1.8 million

Protestors march at the Southwest Ninth Street gate of the Fort Des Moines Army Induction Center in 1967. The July 20 demonstration marked the fourth time in two months that college students opposed to American involvement in the Vietnam War demonstrated there. Courtesy, State Historical Society of Iowa

on light fixtures appropriate to the turn of the century, new sidewalks, and landscaping along Court Avenue.

Public buildings have also been rehabilitated. The Counting Room of the Municipal Building is a glorious collection of ornamental and classical decoration much like its original appearance. The principal courtroom of the U.S. courthouse has received thoughtful renovation. The Public Library of Des Moines again has ornate, gilded stenciling gracing its walls and capitals. And the Polk County Heritage Gallery in the lobby of the former post office (now a county office building) retains its original Art Nouveau and classical designs.

Postwar changes should not be measured exclusively in terms of new construction, nor should it be assumed that successful projects are the only features that describe late twentieth-century Polk County. The boom of construction in metropolitan Des Moines blurs the presence of economic problems in central Iowa. Most center on the farm crisis. In the midst of the agricultural heartland of America, Des Moines and Polk County cannot fail to be touched by falling land values, massive overproduction, and tight credit that has caused farmers to leave their farms in record numbers.

Farm-related business also suffers. Armstrong Tire & Rubber, makers of tractor tires, announced huge layoffs and extracted large wage cuts from the unions. Massey-Ferguson closed its manufacturing operations in the 1980s. Jobs in manufacturing fell in the county from 16 percent in 1975 to 11.7 percent 10 years later. However, farm prices have steadied, and the atmosphere of crisis has lessened.

Other postwar change occurred on the cultural and social fronts. New immigrant groups, barely represented in the immigrations of the previous century,

joined the cultural patchwork that gave Polk County a population of 305,300 in 1980. Latvians fleeing the Soviet takeover of their country have settled in Des Moines. And there are substantial numbers of Des Moines residents with roots in Lebanon, Latin America, Thailand, and Vietnam.

The cycles of change continue to influence the history of Polk County—and without change there would be precious little history to tell. But there is also continuity, threads that weave a portrait of this place. The latest technological innovation in transportation has repeatedly acted as a lightning rod for economic development. Just as the railroads fostered town settlement, the interstates encourage strip development along them. New arrivals continue to enliven the cultural patchwork. Then as now, when local leaders perceive a problem—whether it be the desire to secure the county seat or to bring people downtown—they organize and act to find a solution. When energies are spent and enthusiasm wanes, leaders become complacent or contentious. Cooperation ends, only to begin anew. The cycle of change comes round again in response to new problems and goals.

The local commitment to betterment should "insure a constant accumulation of wealth within its borders." It was so in 1867 when Rufus Blanchard described Polk County that way in his guide to Iowa, and so it remains.

Downtown Des Moines stood poised in 1962 for substantial changes to its skyline. Not yet constructed were such modern landmarks as the Ruan Center, Civic Center, Capital Square, and the Plaza condominiums. The view is to the south, toward the confluence of the Des Moines and Raccoon Rivers where Des Moines began in 1843. Courtesy, Des Moines Pioneer Club

The early twentieth century was clearly the era of brand names and distinctive packaging. Even this small grocery and butcher shop offered such varied carbohydrates as Tip Top Bread, Minnesota Cut-Rite elbow macroni, Crescent vermicelli, Quaker corn flakes, and Roman Meal. Shoppers could also buy Duham's coconut, Bon-Ami cleanser and Fels-Naptha soap. Courtesy, Barbara Beving Long

CHAPTER EIGHT

Partners in Progress

First the Indians gathered at this confluence of two rivers to hunt, fish, and trade with each other. Later the fur traders set up camp there. The military followed, with settlers close behind.

Commerce drove the settlement of this area, and continues to drive it today. As the early farmers needed outlets for their excess production, businesses emerged to meet those needs and provide a market for the farmers' products. Businesses created more business, and a community was born.

Polk County followed a pattern typical of many parts of the state and the nation. The favorable central location attracted the state capital, which created the need for more services and products. Gradually the emphasis turned from agriculture to government and finance. While manufacturing and agriculture have always remained a part of Polk County, commerce, banking, government, and insurance have become dominant in the area.

As Polk County grew in population, more businesses and industries were attracted to it. The influx of people made Polk County the center of the state's population.

The importance of the county to the state and the Midwest has created a burgeoning convention center. While Des Moines has always been a popular site for meetings, the marked expansion of facilities to serve visitors meeting in the city has attracted more and larger conventions in recent years.

The enterprises of Polk County have their own special histories, both short and long. New businesses are created every year; some prosper, others do not, and as time goes by, fledgling businesses become established firms, each with a history that touches thousands of lives both locally and worldwide.

The commercial concerns and civic organizations that have chosen to support the publication of this history book are among the area's oldest and youngest. Some have a heritage going back more than 100 years and have had a great impact on the personality and physical appearance of the city that is their home. These establishments represent a sampling of the many ventures that have taken root and grown in Polk County. They have helped the area to prosper and should be commended for their civic-mindedness and their sense of history.

POLK COUNTY HISTORICAL SOCIETY

The Polk County Historical Society began October 13, 1938, although a similar group was incorporated in 1897. Other than the articles of incorporation, no further information seems to be available about the organization or when it ceased to exist.

Forty-eight charter members formed the current society when articles of incorporation were adopted on December 10, 1938. The first officers were Harvey Ingham, honorary president; Edgar R. Harlan, president; James E. Howard, vice-president; I.H. Tomlinson, secretary; Gladys Bradford, assistant secretary; H.C. Plummer, treasurer; and John A. Wilbois, George R. Wood, and A.A. Reams, trustees.

Harlan was unable to serve as president because of illness and his subsequent relocation to California. On October 14, 1939, Ora Williams was elected president, with Ray C. Stiles as secretary, Gladys Bradford as financial secretary, and Austin C. Graybeal replacing A.A. Reams as a trustee.

At the beginning of World War II the members voted to keep their current officers for the duration of the war. Jonas Poweshiek was elected honorary president for the period of 1942-1943.

Since an insufficient number of members appeared at the annual meeting called for October 6, 1945, no election was held, and the treasurer reported a balance on hand of $5.25. Membership was a constant problem during the early years of the society and attempts to revive it after the war failed, as the official records seem to end at this point.

After some 15 years of inactivity the society was reactivated under the original 1938 articles and bylaws at a meeting held April 17, 1961, at the Iowa State Historical Building. John A. Wilbois, who had been a member of and officer in the society when it was organized, cast the necessary vote to admit the 15 people present as members. Fred S. Pexton, who initiated the revitalization effort, was then elected to serve as temporary chairman.

William D. Houlette presided as temporary chairman at the May 1961 meeting, during which temporary officers were elected to serve until the annual meeting in October. At that time David J. Gonnerman was elected president, and in November three trustees were elected—John A. Wilbois, Fred S. Pexton, and LeRoy G. Pratt.

Regular gatherings continued on a monthly basis at various locations, and by the spring of 1962 membership had increased to 66. The *PCHS Newsletter* was first issued in October of that year by A. Wayne and Florence Keck, who continued the one-page publication at their own expense for six months. In

The 1984 dedication of the initial Polk County flag was held at the historical society's restored cabin. The American flag is a replica of the 26-star flag in use in 1843 when the original Ft. Des Moines was established at this site. Photo by Deane C. Smith

April 1963 Pratt became editor and has served in that capacity ever since, with brief interludes that found the late Georgia M. Reynolds and Woodrow W. Westholm in that position.

Beginning with the annual meeting of October 1962 the following people have held the presidency of the society (the bylaws provide that no officer be elected for more than two consecutive terms in the same office): LeRoy G. Pratt, 1962-1964; Helen Sparks, November to December 1964; R. Louise Pratt, January to October 1965; Howard C. Amick, 1965-1966; Paul K. Ashby, 1966-1968; George S. Holland, 1968-1970; Ole Hellie, 1970-1972; Robert R. Denny, 1972-1974; R. Louise Pratt, 1974-1976; Max Putnam, 1976-1977; Lyle L. Reeves, 1977-1979; Dean C. Stroud, 1979-1981; Reinhold O. Carlson, 1981-1982; James J. Muto, 1982-1983; Deane C. Smith, 1983-1985; Leo Stoll, 1985-1987; James M. Green, 1987-1988; and Ray C. Stiles, son of one of the original 1938 founders, who is currently serving as president.

KDMG-FM

It is a radio station with a short history of existence and an even shorter history in Des Moines. But KDMG-FM 103 has done very well in the Des Moines/central Iowa market with its All Gold format. KDMG plays music whose time has come again. The station has a strict commercial policy that limits advertising to no more than 10 minutes per hour.

KDMG began operations in Pella, southeast of Des Moines, on August 1, 1976. The 100,000-watt transmitter remains in Pella, but station operations and the broadcast studio were moved to Des Moines when a North Carolina company purchased the station on April 1, 1986. The owner, Beta Broadcasting, believed there was room in the Des Moines market for an All Gold hits format.

The employees of KDMG-FM take great pride in the station being the only Des Moines broadcaster located in a building on the National Register of Historic Places—100 Court Avenue. Recently renovated, the building accommodates a number of prestigious firms. It originally housed Warfield, Pratt, Howell Company, a wholesale grocery operation. During Des Moines' expansion years, from 1880 to 1925, the Court Avenue area was dominated by wholesale and retail grocers and related food industries.

Warfield and Howell brought their wholesale grocery business from Illinois to Des Moines in 1880 and moved to this site four years later.

KDMG-FM studios are housed in the historic 100 Court Avenue building, which at one time housed a wholesale grocery firm.

William Pratt joined the firm in 1897. Rapid expansion and a promising future led to the construction of the six-story building in 1902. Three bays added to the building's east side in 1909 completed the structure we see today.

A 1976 survey of historic architecture conducted by the City of Des Moines identified 100 Court Avenue as being the finest architectural styled building in the Court Avenue Historic Area. It is the city's best example of the commercial style of architecture popularized first in the Chicago area between 1875 and 1915, and owing its fame to such great architects as William LeBaron Jenney and Louis Sullivan.

On May 15, 1985, 100 Court Avenue was entered in the National Register of Historic Places.

ALLIED GROUP

After a series of meetings in early spring, 1929, John Evans, B. Rees Jones, and Harry F. Gross, three prominent Iowa mutual insurance executives, saw a need for a service-minded mutual insurance organization that could take care of the casualty needs of mutual insurance agents and their policyholders. Jones, of Town Mutual Dwelling Insurance Company, was elected chairman of the board of directors; Gross, of the Iowa Mutual Tornado Insurance Association, was elected treasurer; Evans, of Poweshiek County Mutual, was elected president; and Wesley Johnson of Dayton, secretary of the Scandinavian Mutual Fire and Lightning Association, was elected secretary.

Other directors elected were J.E. Brooks of Greenfield, secretary of Adair County Mutual; O.K. Maben, secretary of the Farmers Mutual Fire and Lightning Association of Hancock County; J.L. Fober, president of the Cascade Farmers Mutual Fire Association; William Treimer, secretary of O'Brien County Mutual; P.J. Shaw, secretary of Pocahantas County Mutual; O.A. McKinney of Davenport; and J. Lindley Coon of Cedar Rapids.

The name of the newly formed company: Allied Mutual Automobile Association. The directors believed the name

Allied Group president John E. Evans is the grandson of company founder John Evans.

Company cars are lined up outside the firm's first building in 1949. This location is also the site of the current headquarters.

should reflect the firm's origin—the combined efforts of several organizations.

With a $50 contribution from each of the directors, the company was on its way. On March 25, 1929, Allied Mutual Automobile Association was granted an insurance charter and, on April 1, 1929, wrote its first three policies to its three founders. A Certificate of Authority was received from the state of Iowa on May 10, 1929.

One of the firm's early accomplishments was a first in the insurance field: the offering of farm liability policies to farmers in the early 1940s. The company entered the workers' compensation field in 1941.

In the beginning business was conducted out of a rented room in the Hubbell Building. In 1949 construction was completed on new quarters at 700 Fourth. Ultimately, the growth would call for 75 percent more floor space by 1959, a major addition in 1969-1970, and additional stories in 1975.

In 1939 some 75,000 Iowa State Fairgoers flocked into Allied Mutual's exhibit of two dual-control cars purchased for Iowa field personnel to promote safe driving. Concerned with greater highway safety and the reduction of accidents, Allied distributed more than 45,000 safe-driver pamphlets to inquiring motorists at the fair. The company claimed to be the first automobile insurance company to use dual-control cars as a permanent part of its equipment.

In 1940 the organization's name was changed to Allied Mutual Casualty Company. Soon recognized as a leading multiple-line insurance firm, Allied

During the 1939 Iowa State Fair, 75,000 fairgoers were treated to a look at Allied's dual-control driver-training cars—a first for an Iowa casualty company.

After a variety of additions and expansions, the home office on Fifth Street has been modernized with this striking entrance.

Mutual expanded its services in 1959 with the creation of AMCO Insurance Company, a provider of fire and casualty insurance for specialized lines. With an increase in property and casualty writings in 1960, another name change occurred. The firm was now called Allied Mutual Insurance Company.

A consolidation with Town Mutual Dwelling Insurance Company of Des Moines in 1961 marked a major augmentation to the growth of the Allied companies. From the mid-1960s through the mid-1970s, Allied Mutual expanded westward with the acquisition of five companies: in Iowa, Iowa Home Mutual Casualty Company; in Nebraska, Standard Reliance Insurance Company; in Idaho, Snake River Mutual Insurance Company; and in California, Sierra Mutual Fire Insurance Company and Farmers Mutual Insurance Company of Santa Rosa.

Leading the firm through this time of rapid expansion was John E. Evans, current president, named to that office in 1963. Evans is grandson of founder and former president John Evans, and son of Harold S. Evans, who headed the company from 1936 through 1959.

The AMCO Insurance Company was the first to file with the Iowa Insurance Department to write Dram Shop Liability coverage (liquor liability) following passage of enabling legislation in 1963.

The organization of Allied Life Insurance Company in 1965 marked its entrance into the life insurance field with a wide range of individual and family protection contracts.

An extensive corporate identification study in 1968 prompted the firm to select one single identity, AID Insurance Services, to encompass all of its services. The word AID was selected as representative of the basic services offered by an insurance company.

However, in 1986, national attention to the viral infection known as Acquired Immune Deficiency Syndrome (AIDS) clouded the corporate identity. The organization thus renamed itself ALLIED Group.

Today, what began as a small insurance company has grown into a variety of firms with numerous markets and services. Property and casualty insurance is the mainstay of the company's business, with a marketing territory of 14 states served by four regional offices. The parent corporation, ALLIED Mutual Insurance Company, has two main divisions—ALLIED Group, Inc., a downstream holding company with partial public ownership, and AID Finance, which is made up of ALLIED Crop Agency, Inc., and ALLIED Securities Corporation, a full-service broker/dealer in financial securities.

Under ALLIED Group, Inc., is ALLIED Life Insurance Company with its subsidiary, ALLIED Life Brokerage Agency, Inc. Also under the ALLIED Group, Inc., umbrella is ALLIED Property and Casualty Insurance Company, which markets through agencies with special exclusive personal lines contracts; Depositors Insurance Company, which markets through agencies of financial institutions; Western Heritage Insurance Company, located in Phoenix, Arizona, an excess and surplus lines insurance company; and ALLIED Group Leasing Corporation, which handles automobile and equipment leasing.

Special property and casualty lines are handled by AMCO Insurance Company. Subsidiaries include ALLIED Group Mortgage Company, which arranges home-mortgage loans; ALLIED Group Information Systems, Inc., which markets computer services to insurance organizations; and King Management Company, an investment and farm management firm with two associated farm realty offices—Don Knudsen Realty, Inc., and Sandage Real Estate Inc. Also under AMCO is ALLIED General Agency Company, an excess and surplus lines agency.

IOWA METHODIST MEDICAL CENTER

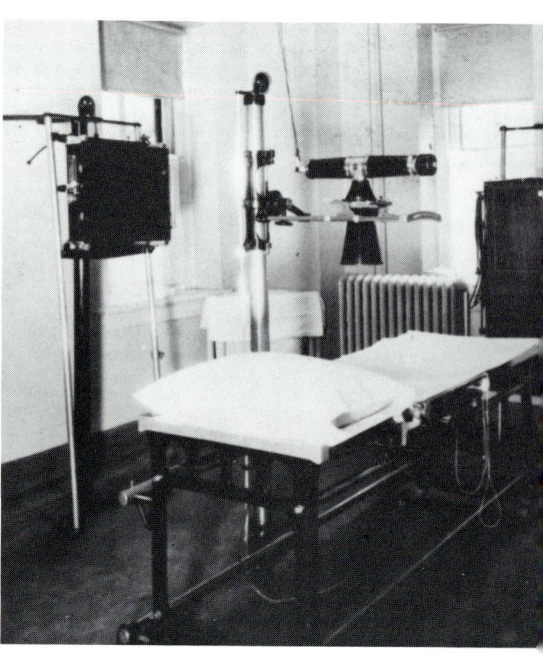

The east wing was added to the Callanan Building in 1912. The new addition housed operating rooms, the new X-ray (above) and orthopedic departments, and a pathology laboratory.

At the turn of the century a small red-brick institution called Callanan College stood on a quiet hill overlooking downtown Des Moines and the valleys of the Des Moines and Raccoon rivers. This serene environment would ultimately evolve into Iowa's largest private health care facility—Iowa Methodist Medical Center.

On January 16, 1901, after the United Methodist Conference purchased the three-acre academic institution from its founder, James Callanan, Iowa Methodist Hospital opened its doors at 1200 Pleasant Street. On that historic day six patients were admitted to the new hospital, which could accommodate up to 30 patients.

Thirty beds were too few. By May of the first year 54 patients were causing the hospital walls to bulge, and cots were brought in. The hospital was bustling with activity and bursting at the seams. Expansion plans were already under way.

In 1903 a new wing was under construction to the west of the Callanan, or central, building. It was completed and dedicated in 1905 to meet the needs of a still-growing patient population.

The early years of Iowa Methodist Hospital saw continuing growth and expansion. An internal telephone system was installed to hasten communications to the doctors and staff. Many doctors were discouraging women from having their babies at home, so an obstetrical unit was established at the hospital. The pharmacy expanded, and an anesthetist was added to the staff.

Just four years after the west wing was completed, a second wing underwent construction to the east and was opened in 1912. The expansion projects quickly proved their worth. Though two years too late to help the space needs created by the typhoid fever epidemic of 1910, the east wing helped patients of the smallpox epidemic three years later, a severe influenza epidemic in 1918, and a diphtheria outbreak in 1919.

The period between 1910 and 1920 was not an easy one for the hospital. When the United States formally declared war in April 1917, the hospital and its nurses, attendants, and facilities were promptly placed at the disposal of the government. World War I created a shortage of nurses and interns while the patient population remained high. In addition, the hospital provided physicals for applicants enrolling in the Officers Reserve Corps of the Army.

In 1911 the first X-ray machine was purchased. It was "a wonderful new instrument that could see right through the patient," said a member of the 1914 nursing class. Even then technology was improving so quickly that the X-ray equipment was outmoded and replaced in a few years. Just 20 years after its opening, Iowa Methodist Hospital was approved by the American College of Surgeons.

The Iowa Methodist School of Nursing, which graduated its first class of four nurses in 1903, had grown to 122 students by 1924. The school was already considered one of the finest nursing schools and was recognized as the second-largest Methodist nursing school in the country.

The Great Depression had crippling effects on Iowa Methodist and

PARTNERS IN PROGRESS

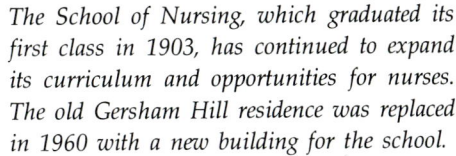

The School of Nursing, which graduated its first class in 1903, has continued to expand its curriculum and opportunities for nurses. The old Gersham Hill residence was replaced in 1960 with a new building for the school.

Iowa's only hospital dedicated to the treatment of children was opened in 1944 as the Raymond Blank Memorial Hospital for Children.

the patients it served. While tremendous advances in medical technology were being made, the hospital struggled to maintain the high-level services, technology, and personnel despite cutbacks in pay and a reduction in the School of Nursing program.

The increasing need for special services for children led to the establishment of the Raymond Blank Memorial Hospital for Children in 1944. Generous contributions from Mr. and Mrs. A.H. Blank made possible the hospital, named in memory of their son who died in early adulthood. The hospital grew from 70 to 112 beds, and during the polio epidemic of 1948 to 1950, every bed was needed.

In 1951 yet another wing of the hospital was opened to the south of the reconstructed Callanan Building. It housed the first psychiatric service in any general hospital in Iowa and an all-new pharmacy. The first open-heart surgery in the country outside of Rochester, Minnesota, was performed at Iowa Methodist in 1956.

During the 1950s construction of the eight-story Younker Memorial Rehabilitation Center began, and the Poison Information Center was established.

Central Iowa's only radiation-therapy department, at Iowa Methodist, administered the first cobalt-therapy treatment in 1962. Ten years later a new linear accelerator was activated to supplement the cobalt-therapy service for radiation therapy.

Since the first open-heart surgery in 1956, Iowa Methodist has been considered a leader in cardiac care and rehabilitation. The cardiac rehabilitation program enables physicians to precisely evaluate the tolerance of the heart and vascular systems. An important result has been the reduction from nine to seven days of hospital stay by the average cardiac patient.

In 1975 Iowa Methodist Hospital changed its name to Iowa Methodist Medical Center to reflect the many new areas of medical service. The hospital—with its central building; east, west, and south wings; and Blank Children's Hospital—had already expanded to more than 24 acres. It has added the Younker Memorial Rehabilitation Center, a new School of Nursing building, a cafeteria building, the Helen Powell Convalescent Center, the Pleasant Hill Nursing Center, and a five-story North Wing, which today stands nine stories.

Today Iowa Methodist has spread far beyond its 42-acre campus. Outreach programs have added convenience and more cost-effective medical services to the community; three Iowa Methodist Neighborhood Clinics provide medical care to patients on a walk-in basis seven days a week; an off-campus outpatient surgery center, Day Surgery of West Des Moines, offers 300 surgical procedures on a same-day basis; an Iowa Methodist Executive Fitness Center provides the most thorough physical exams available for business executives; the Iowa Methodist Sports Medicine Center offers conditioning and rehabilitation services to area athletes; and the Iowa Methodist Nutrition Center provides guidance in nutrition and weight-reduction programs.

From small beginnings back in 1901, when the institution opened its doors to its first six patients, Iowa Methodist Medical Center has evolved into the largest private medical center in the state.

Iowa Methodist's Life Flight helicopter ambulance went into service in 1979. Currently Life Flight serves 58 counties in central Iowa.

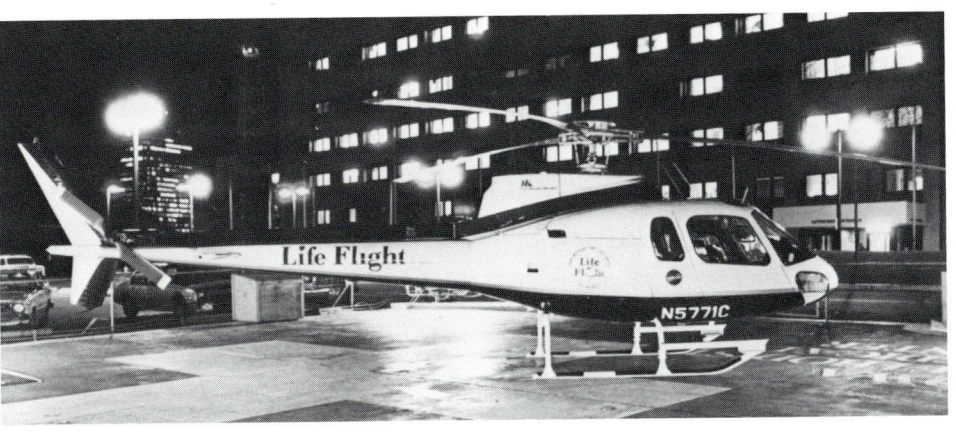

EMPLOYERS MUTUAL CASUALTY COMPANY

The Employers Mutual Group of Companies began in 1911 as the Employers Mutual Casualty Association of Iowa to write workers' compensation insurance. The guiding force behind the new association was John A. Gunn.

Gunn had served as president of the Iowa Manufacturers Association, a group that played a significant role in the formation of Employers Mutual. He was a strong-willed, no-nonsense man who worked to establish an investment policy of selecting high-grade state and municipal bonds.

More accurately, however, the association was organized to fill an immediate need: The company was incorporated in March 1911 and wrote its first policies in 1912 before the Iowa workers' compensation laws became effective July 1, 1914.

Before these laws went into effect, times were rough for the injured worker. He received nothing when hurt at work unless he sued his employer, and then he had to prove that the injury was the direct result of the employer's negligence. Even if he won a suit against his employer, there were no prescribed awards for specific injuries; the amount of the award depended largely on the discretion of a jury.

Employers Mutual was able to offer coverage cheaper than the eastern companies that serviced the Midwest through general agencies, which in turn serviced local agencies.

In 1924 the name of the firm was changed to Employers Mutual Casualty Company. Shortly thereafter, the firm expanded into other lines of insurance. Though the company's activities were originally limited to Iowa, it eventually moved into surrounding states where many clients had branches or plants.

Promising as this growth might seem, however, the firm also had its share of problems. A major obstacle was the opposition from the stock companies and their agents who denounced mutual companies as socialistic and financially unsound.

This difficulty was eventually overcome, and today Employers Mutual is one of the largest writers of workers' compensation in Iowa. It has also become the largest Iowa-based fire, casualty, and bonding company.

Employers Mutual was founded in Des Moines, where its home office remains, and today holds licenses in all 50 states and the District of Columbia. Approximately 75 percent of the firm's business and 56 percent of its employees work outside of Iowa. The company now provides about 100 different kinds of insurance coverage, including workers' compensation.

Despite its economic outreach into other states, Employers Mutual remains active in many Des Moines and civic endeavors. Many civic functions take place in the spacious lobby of its home office. The company has also provided office space to the

John A. Gunn (left) served as president and guiding force behind Employers Mutual Casualty Association when it was founded in 1911.

The tall lighted building (below) in the background is corporate headquarters for the Employers Mutual Group of Companies with the Des Moines Branch Office Building in the foreground. A portion of the Employers Modern Life Company is visible in the left background.

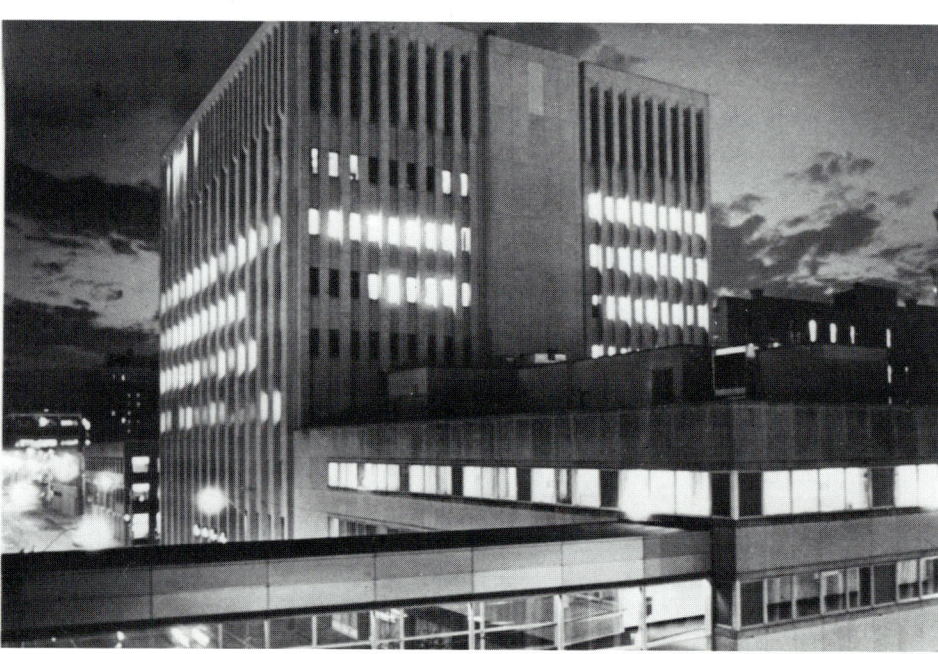

PARTNERS IN PROGRESS

Des Moines Symphony and to the area intergovernmental survey group, Public Service Research, Inc. Employers Mutual had made significant contributions toward the redevelopment of downtown Des Moines, and endowed an insurance professorship at Drake University.

The Employers Mutual of today is the parent company of what is often called Employers Mutual Companies, or the Employers Mutual Group. There are 9 insurance companies in the group, some of which are owned by Employers Mutual and others of which are owned by a downstream holding company, EMC Insurance Group Inc., which is a publicly held stock company. Employers Mutual owns a majority interest, approximately 65 percent, of the stock of the public company.

The old home office building before the 1956 expansion that extended left to the corner.

A composite photograph shows company officers and a new billboard that started an outdoor advertising campaign, circa 1963.

THE WEITZ COMPANY, INC.

Charles Weitz emigrated to America in 1850 and opened his contracting business in Des Moines in 1855. Shortly after the turn of the century Weitz launched Century Lumber Company as a separate business. Charles Weitz Sons occupied this site from 1886 until 1942, replacing this office at 713 Mulberry with a five-story building in the late 1920s.

In 1854 Charles Weitz, a carpenter who had come to the United States from Germany in 1850, read in a Columbus, Ohio, newspaper that the capital of Iowa was to be moved from Iowa City to Fort Des Moines. The following spring he and his wife, with their household possessions in a prairie schooner drawn by two mules, arrived in the little town of Fort Des Moines.

Charles Weitz, Builder & Contractor, was headquartered at 119 Third Street. His first job was putting windows in the basement of the old Savery House where the Kirkwood Hotel now stands. His first contract to build was for a drugstore on Second Street, with "inside trim of black walnut." Thus was founded what is believed to be the oldest construction firm west of the Mississippi and the oldest continuous business under family management in Des Moines, and perhaps, Iowa.

Weitz is believed by some to have built the first city hall in 1882 at Second and Locust streets, although company records cannot substantiate the claim. But it is known that the firm built the present city hall in 1910 at a low bid of $301,960. Charles Weitz also built many of the original Fort Des Moines buildings in the 1890s.

When Weitz died in 1906, he was president of the German Savings Bank and a charter member and director of Valley National Bank. In 1903 his sons—Frederick, Charles, and Edward—had taken over the business as a partnership under the firm name of Charles Weitz Sons, with Frederick Weitz assuming the leading role. The Century Lumber Company, also owned by the Weitz family, was directed by Charles and Edward Weitz. It was liquidated in 1952.

During this period the firm built such landmarks as the Hubbell Building in 1914, the Valley National Bank Building in 1916 (on the site of Capital Square), the Hotel Fort Des Moines in 1918, and the Wallace Homestead Plant, Hoyt Sherman Place Auditorium, and the Drake University Fieldhouse and Stadium in the 1920s.

The name of the firm was changed in 1933 to The Weitz Company, Inc., and, after the death of Frederick Weitz in 1935, Rudolph as president and Heinrich as vice-president became the third generation of management. During the Great Depression the firm built post offices nationwide. In fact, it has built post office buildings in 42 states.

The company also played an important role in military installations. As the managing partner of joint ventures, it was responsible for the Camp Dodge

The present city hall was built by Weitz in 1910 at a low bid of $301,960.

When Weitz opened the Wakonda Court apartments (top right) in the fall of 1951, there was little development that far south. Today the complex is surrounded by later development.

One of the grain-storage facilities (above) designed by Weitz in East Pakistan (now Bangladesh). These facilities helped ease the famine by providing storage for the grain shipped from all over the world.

Cantonment in World War I and the Des Moines Ordnance Plant (now John Deere) during World War II.

Well-known buildings constructed by The Weitz Company during the post-World War II period include an addition to the *Register & Tribune* building, the Iowa Power and Light office building, Drake University dormitories, and the Solar plant (later occupied by Massey-Ferguson).

During the 1960s The Weitz Company acquired a Kansas City firm specializing in grain-storage facilities. Rudolph Weitz personally promoted modern food-storage around the world, and the company performed distribution studies and/or engineering designs for Egypt, Brazil, Argentina, Colombia, Nicaragua, Guyana, Pakistan, Indonesia, the West Africa Entente States, Honduras, and the Philippines. Its work on storage facilities in East Pakistan played a pivotal role following the revolution and establishment of Bangladesh. Those facilities made it possible to move grain into the country during the upheaval and resulting famine.

In 1963 Frederick W. Weitz II, Rudolph's son, became the fourth generation of the family to direct the organization. Rudolph, active in community affairs, continued to serve as chairman of the board until his death in 1974.

Familiar projects during this period include the new post office, the Employers Mutual Building, three downtown buildings for Northwestern Bell, Hoover High School, the Des Moines Art Center Sculpture Court, Federal Home Loan Bank, and the Des Moines Civic Center.

In 1961 Weitz became involved in the development and construction of retirement home communities. This business steadily grew until, in 1971, Life Care Services Corporation was formed to operate as a company specializing in developing, building, and managing retirement home projects. Today more than 50 life-care retirement facilities have been planned, developed, or managed in locations across the United States.

Growth and expansion outside Des Moines led to the creation of branch offices in Phoenix, Arizona; West Palm Beach, Florida; and the Boston area. In 1986 a Denver-based construction firm, Al Cohen Construction Company, merged its general contracting services with The Weitz Company, Inc.

Recent notable Des Moines area projects include Locust Mall, Capital Square, the Hub Tower, and Kaleidoscope at the Hub, and construction in the Drake University area of the Old Main apartments, Drake Inn, Drake Court apartments, and the Drake Legal Clinic. Additional projects include a new broadcasting facility for Iowa Public Television in Johnston, the new historical building for the State of Iowa, Tower Medical Clinic for University of Osteopathic Medicine and Health Sciences, the Regency West Office Park in West Des Moines, and the Central Iowa Racetrack in Altoona.

UNIVERSITY OF OSTEOPATHIC MEDICINE & HEALTH SCIENCES

The story of the University of Osteopathic Medicine & Health Sciences is one of continuous progress. At the time of its founding in 1898 as the Dr. S.S. Still College of Osteopathy, miracle medicines and sure-cure treatments pervaded the health care field. Osteopathic medicine turned away from such treatments, advocating that good health depended upon the proper functioning of all body systems rather than upon the administration of massive doses of non-specific drugs.

Osteopathic medicine traces its origins to the post-Civil War era, when Andrew Taylor Still, M.D., defected from the medical practice of his time and promulgated osteopathy as an alternative philosophy of medical care. Dr. Still insisted that the medical practice of his day was usually ineffective—often inhuman and needlessly painful. He was barred from teaching his new philosophy in medical institutions of the day. As a result, he founded the first school of osteopathic medicine at Kirksville, Missouri, in 1892.

Dr. S.S. Still, founder of the university.

The differences between osteopathic medicine and allopathic medicine are subtle, yet significant. One of the most consequential differences is the emphasis on the art and science of palpatory diagnosis and manipulative therapy, which osteopathic physicians use in concert with all other advances of modern therapeutics. In addition, the osteopathic physician emphasizes the inter-relationship of the musculoskeletal system, the autonomic nervous system, and the circulatory and lymphatic systems of the body in health, dysfunction, and disease.

Still College was founded in Des Moines in 1898 by S.S. Still, nephew of Andrew Taylor Still. The college was housed in a single building at 1422 Locust Street in Des Moines, where it offered a two-year course of instruction. In the years that followed, the curriculum was lengthened to three, and later four, years. In 1927 the college acquired larger facilities on Sixth Avenue.

In the early 1940s the name was changed to the Des Moines Still College of Osteopathy and Surgery to better describe its total curriculum. A College Hospital was acquired, and the first ambulatory clinic building was purchased to provide more opportunities for the training of students in clinical medicine.

The Locust Street home of the college at approximately the turn of the century.

The Azneer Academic Center has administrative offices, three lecture halls, the library, and the university museum.

Dr. J. Leonard Azneer, current president, greets graduates at the annual commencement.

The Tower Medical Clinic is the newest addition to the university campus.

In 1958 the institution was renamed the College of Osteopathic Medicine and Surgery. With the acquisition of 24 acres of land at Fort Des Moines, the first satellite clinic was established in 1963. In 1971 the Dietz Diagnostic Center was opened at the Fort Des Moines location to serve as a major outpatient clinic. It also served as the first college specialty clinic.

In 1972 the college expanded its campus and teaching facilities by moving to its present 22-acre site on Grand Avenue. The new campus has enabled the college to gradually increase its enrollment from 115 to 175 students in each entering class.

The expansion of the didactic teaching program was complemented by the establishment of additional clinics in Des Moines and outlying communities that are served by faculty and senior students who provide vital medical services to the public while participating in valuable learning experiences.

In 1980 the board of trustees voted to make the college a true university with the establishment of the College of Podiatric Medicine and Surgery and the College of Biological Sciences. These two join the College of Osteopathic Medicine and Surgery as the University of Osteopathic Medicine and Health Sciences. Fall 1987 enrollment totaled 1,046 full-time and 36 part-time students.

The College of Podiatric Medicine and Surgery offers a four-year curriculum of podiatric medical education leading to the Doctor of Podiatric Medicine (D.P.M.) degree. The college, which enrolled its first class in August 1982, is the only podiatric college in the nation that is part of a health science university. The college operates five podiatric clinics in Iowa, Missouri, and Minnesota.

The College of Biological Sciences awards the bachelor of science (B.S.) degree in biological sciences for completion of the physician assistant program, the master of science (M.S.) and bachelor of science (B.S.) degrees in health care administration, the master of science (M.S.) degree in physical therapy, and the bachelor of science (B.S.) degree in health information management.

The university opened the Tower Medical Clinic on campus in early 1987. The 10-story, $15-million tower offers primary care, medical specialties, and ambulatory surgery. It serves as a regional referral center for the osteopathic profession. Attached to the Tower are the 1,500-seat Olsen Medical Education Center and a three-level parking ramp.

With an eye toward helping meet increased demands for better trained health professionals and achieving better distribution of medical services, the university is among the pacesetters in the current trends of medical education and practice in the nation. As it approaches its 10th decade, the University of Osteopathic Medicine & Health Sciences reaffirms its commitment to educate primary health care providers for Iowa and the nation.

MID-AMERICA GROUP, LTD.

The history of Mid-America Group, Ltd., reflects the entrepreneurial spirit of its founder, Marvin A. Pomerantz. A Des Moines native, Pomerantz founded Great Plains Bag Corporation, a producer of paper and polyethylene bags, in 1961. As the company grew, there was need for additional space. New warehouses were built, used, and then leased by a long-term tenant. Pomerantz would then build another facility. The realty company became Mid-America Development Company in 1972 and proceeded to expand on Pomerantz' idea—erect a building suitable for a variety of uses, fill it, lease it, and build again.

Great Plains Bag Corporation became a subsidiary of the Continental Group, Inc., and in 1972 Pomerantz was named vice-president of Continental Can Company, Inc. In January 1973 he was named vice-president and general manager of the Forest Products Brown Systems operation, a significant segment of Continental's organization. Pomerantz left Continental in 1976 to pursue his property development interests.

Mid-America's success is based upon quality construction and versatility. The company used steel frames, brick and concrete, and flexible cubage in amassing nearly one million square feet of leased warehouse and industrial space. Design versatility enabled the firm to build desirable space with no advance idea of the eventual tenant.

Marvin Pomerantz (above left), the guiding force behind Mid-America, speaks at a birthday celebration for longtime Des Moines Diocese Bishop Maurice Dingman.

When Mid-America Development Company built a property, Mid-America Warehousing would lease the space and serve such clients as Firestone, Monsanto, and others. Later the buildings would be customized to fit the needs of the long-term lessee.

The development of the multibuilding Mid-America Industrial Park began in the early 1970s and now has approximately 300,000 square feet of prime industrial space at 63rd and Park Avenue in Des Moines. Mid-America now has nearly 2 million square feet of industrial and office space.

In the mid-1970s Mid-America Development Company began undertaking joint ventures on build-to-suit projects, including the company's association with local architects in the Westridge Office Park in West Des Moines; a joint venture project for Northwestern Bell's Des Moines work center; a partnership for an office building in Colorado Springs, Colorado; and a joint venture agreement for the Waterfall Glen Office park in the Chicago area.

Mid-America also continues to develop commercial and residential

Chauchuc Grid (above), a sculpture fulfilled by water, was created by Scopia to highlight the plaza adjacent to Regency West 3 and 4.

land. Land zoned for single-family homes is developed into attractive neighborhoods complete with public streets, utility lines, and parks. These lots are then sold to builders with covenants dictating land use and construction.

While continuing to develop residential land and warehouse sites, Mid-America has placed an emphasis on developing high-quality office buildings. Mid-America's 11th office building is under construction, and the philosophy of creating campus environments that attract quality companies for long-term leases continues. Westridge, with its three buildings—Agri, Equitable, and Mid-America—was among the first in the area to apply this concept. Today this approach is continued at the 44-acre Regency West complex in West Des Moines.

Regency West will include eight buildings. Seven of these buildings are currently in use, and one is under construction for occupancy in 1989. The buildings reflect award-winning style, extremely flexible interior treatments, and state-of-the-art communications and telecommunications systems. The buildings are sited with open spaces, sculpture, and pedestrian

PARTNERS IN PROGRESS

walkways. The interiors reflect the emphasis on quality with fine carpeting, oak, and chrome trim.

The unique shared communications and data-management system serving the complex is connected to national and international AT&T network services. In addition, tenants are able to realize support and management time savings through the personalized call-processing and message-delivery service provided by the Regency West Electronic Message Center.

A sophisticated meeting facility provides Iowa's first interactive video teleconferencing in a fully managed, comfortable conference room environment. This facility provides clients a uniquely cost-efficient and effective way to meet with colleagues across the country or around the world.

Marvin Pomerantz is chairman and chief executive officer of Gaylord Container Corporation, and Mid-America Group, Ltd., with approximately 3,500 employees in approximately 30 locations throughout the United States. In addition, he continues to be deeply involved in community and state affairs, and currently serves as president of the State Board of Regents that oversees Iowa's public universities and other educational facilities.

Some subsidiaries of Mid-America Group, Ltd., are Mid-America Development Company, Mid-America Investment Co., Mid-America Property, Inc., Mid-America Warehousing, Inc., and Mid-America Transportation Inc.

Growth, a Scopia sculpture (top) gracing the Westridge Office Park.

The Regency West video teleconferencing room (center) offers high-tech opportunity for worldwide communications.

Mid-America and Financial Information Trust officials break ground (right) for Regency West 7—the new home of the Trust.

AMERICAN MUTUAL LIFE

Back before the turn of the century fraternal associations were popular social centers in rural and small-town America. The associations provided an outlet for activity in a time before the automobile, radio, or movie theater.

The Brotherhood of American Yeomen (forerunner of American Mutual Life) was organized in Bancroft, Iowa, and incorporated under the laws of the state on December 27, 1897. The monthly dues supported the administration of the organization and, as a fringe benefit, provided $500 or $1,000 of life insurance coverage to each member.

The Brotherhood of American Yeomen got its name, the title of its officers, its uniforms, and its rituals from the story of *Ivanhoe* by Sir Walter Scott. The original organizers were energetic and enthusiastic, and by 1917 had helped the fraternity grow to nearly 300,000 members.

During the 1920s interest in the fraternal form of social organization began to wane rapidly, a process that

The neon lights atop the American Mutual Life Building (above) are a landmark in downtown Des Moines.

seems to have continued for many fraternals to this day. The leaders of the Yeomen decided to separate the insurance operation entirely from the organization and carry it on as a regular mutual life insurance company. The insurance operation remained in the Yeomen's office building near the area now occupied by Veterans Memorial Auditorium.

The Yeomen Mutual was formed in 1932 in Des Moines, its name changed to American Mutual Life in 1938.

During the Depression years of the 1930s the company had little growth in volume of business in force. Although the Depression was a challenge to company leadership, the firm emerged from those testing times in excellent financial condition.

The real growth of American Mutual Life began in 1946 at the end of World War II. The influx of returning servicemen, the increase in the number of families, and related family responsibilities created a favorable climate for the insurance industry. Since that time American Mutual Life has seen the amount of protection provided its policy owners grow from $90 million to more than $7 billion.

In the late 1940s the company moved into downtown Des Moines, occupying space at Sixth and Grand. The lighted neon signs on top of the building at the east and north sides have become downtown landmarks.

American Mutual Life currently has 1,500 sales representatives working in 30 states. Assets of $500 million and total surplus in excess of $100 million have given the company national prominence. The firm continues to receive the highest rating of "A+ Superior" from Best's, an independent rating agency.

The current officers of American Mutual Life are Sam C. Kalainov, CLU, chairman of the board and chief executive officer; William R. Engel, president and treasurer; William E. McGrath, CLU, senior vice-president/marketing; James J. Streck, FSA, senior vice-president/insurance operations and secretary; Larry E. Dybvad, CLU, vice-president/agency; Robert C. Fay, vice-president/investments; Jerry L. Koppen, FLMI, vice-president/data processing; John E. Mechem, FLMI, vice-president and comptroller; and Ronald P. Wittenwyler, FSA, vice-president and actuary.

American Mutual's predecessor company, Yeomen Mutual Life (below), was located in this building near the site of Veterans Memorial Auditorium.

PITT-DES MOINES, INC.

When he designed a steel tower to replace the old wooden-style water towers, William H. Jackson was some six years ahead of the competition. He was 24 years old, a recent civil engineering graduate from Iowa State College, and Fort Madison's first city engineer.

It was 1892, and he saw the time was right for new towns in the Midwest to expand and develop. He formed a partnership with a college friend, B.N. Moss, and went into the waterworks field to design and construct those new products.

He located a fabricator for his steel tanks in Pittsburgh, Pennsylvania—the Keystone Bridge Company (American Bridge Company). Jackson's improvement in the material, design, and construction of water towers made it easier for the new company to secure contracts.

Moss and Jackson spent the next few years traveling to towns, building and contracting for local water systems. By 1900 most wooden tanks were being replaced by steel. But the freight cost of fabricating the steel towers in Pittsburgh was becoming prohibitive.

E.W. Crellin, who owned a small Des Moines fabricating plant, joined Moss and Jackson in forming the Des Moines Bridge and Iron Company, a partnership. A corporation, the Des Moines Bridge and Iron Works, was formed to take the steel from Pittsburgh and perform the actual fabrication, while the partnership sold the jobs and erected them. Jackson and Moss each put up $4,000, and Crellin contributed his plant, located on Tuttle Street from Ninth to 11th. It would remain the base of operations in Des Moines. The company manufactured bridges, water tanks, waterworks, and electric lighting plants.

In 1907 Jackson located a site in Pittsburgh near the steel mills where he soon erected a plant. By 1910 he had moved the firm's headquarters to this location on Neville Island near Pittsburgh.

Administrative offices and the fabricating plant have remained at the Tuttle Street location in Des Moines. In 1955 a modern plate structure plant was built on 80 acres in Clive, a northwest suburb of Des Moines. In 1964 the Des Moines Steel Company, an independent fabricator a few blocks from the Tuttle location, was acquired as a subsidiary.

In 1916 the firm's name was changed to Pittsburgh-Des Moines Steel Company (a partnership) and the corporation became Pittsburgh-Des Moines Company. Moss left the business around 1905; Crellin remained president until 1923, when Jackson bought his interest; and in 1956 the partnership was dissolved and a single corporation, Pittsburgh-Des Moines Steel Company, emerged.

Jackson died in 1939, and his son, John E., became president. A younger son, William R., became president and chief executive officer in 1959, and John E. became chairman of the board. After John E. died in 1971, Thomas W. Fauntleroy became president and William R. became chairman of the board.

The 3-million-gallon hydropillar fabricated by Pitt-Des Moines and located in Montgomery, Alabama.

The firm has expanded its operations and product lines through additional plants nationwide. Foreign subsidiaries were located in Guatemala, Australia, South America, Saudi Arabia, and Canada.

In recent years the company has moved into new techniques in low-temperature research, cryogenics, space technology for the aerospace industry, high-rise buildings, and other applications. Symbolic of the firm's growth is a comparison of the original water tower to its most famous product—the Gateway Arch in St. Louis.

The current name of the company is Pitt-Des Moines, Inc., and it is listed on the American Stock Exchange.

The Gateway Arch in St. Louis, Missouri, is one of Pitt-Des Moines' most famous achievements.

HOLMES, MURPHY & ASSOCIATES, INC.

Holmes, Murphy & Associates, Inc., was founded in 1932 by Max L. Holmes. With 10 years of experience in the insurance business in Des Moines, he formed his own general agency and guided its growth until his retirement in 1971. He built the foundation for his agency through the sale of life insurance and personal insurance.

In the late 1940s Holmes hired Ray Murphy, Jr., an all-lines insurance salesman. Murphy had been a member of the 1939 University of Iowa "Ironmen" football team and winner of the Big Ten Medal for Academic and Athletic Excellence. Murphy soon became a partner in the firm and, for the next three decades, was the catalyst for the company's development as a leading midwestern commercial property/casualty agency. Murphy also became a prominent community leader, serving as chairman of the Greater Des Moines Chamber of Commerce Federation and co-chairman of the annual United Way drive.

In 1957 the company moved from humble offices in the Hubbell Building into its own facility at 1022 High Street. Enlarged and remodeled several times, the building was eventually reconstructed to provide an expansion of more than 10,000 square feet in 1974.

Holmes Murphy changed its business structure from a partnership to a corporation in 1971, and Murphy was elected president. Under his leadership the company grew to a staff of 42 employees and revenues exceeding $3 million.

Murphy succumbed to a year-long battle with cancer in 1978 at the age of 60. The company and the community lost an outstanding leader. Robert Dee, who had been executive vice-president, was elected president and holds that position today. Dee has continued Murphy's role in community and industry leadership. In 1984 he was elected chairman of the Greater Des Moines Chamber of Commerce Federation, making Holmes Murphy one of the few firms in the city to have had two top executives elected to this position.

Today major fields of operation consist of commercial and industrial insurance, contractors' insurance and bonding, and association group, life, accident and health, pension, profit-sharing, and personal insurance. Holmes Murphy regularly contracts with 21 major insurance companies, but has access to virtually every insurance market in the world.

In 1983 the firm found it necessary to provide more space for its growing operation. The employee benefit department had already been moved to an office at 1100 High Street, and in July of that year it acquired the Higgs Warnock Palis Agency of Des Moines. The Interstate Assurance Company building at 420 Keo Way became available and was purchased as the third location for the company. The three-story, 36,000-square-foot building was completely remodeled to fit the organization's needs.

The firm now has more than 100 employees and revenues exceeding $11 million. *Business Insurance Magazine* recently ranked the company 48th out of some 6,000 insurance agencies and brokerage houses nationwide.

The most recent expansion came in 1987, when the firm opened its first branch office in Dallas, Texas. With many clients operating, not only in Texas, but in many cities throughout the United States, Holmes, Murphy & Associates, Inc., may well be opening more branches in other parts of the country.

In the summer of 1984 Holmes Murphy employees gathered in front of their new home at 420 Keo Way.

HERITAGE COMMUNICATIONS, INC.

The youthful founders of Heritage Communications (above, left to right), James Hoak, Jr., and James Cownie.

Heritage moved into this location (left) in the late 1970s, later adding an addition on the far end.

An idea born over lunch at a local restaurant started two young men then in their twenties on a path that has led their company to phenomenal success. That day in 1970 James Hoak and James Cownie discussed the bid by a cable television company to bring cable service to Des Moines.

They decided there was a lot of opportunity in the cable area and that they wanted to be a part of it. Through contacts in the Des Moines business community, money was raised and Heritage Communications, Inc., was incorporated. In 1971 its initial public offering of $1.275 million in stock was completed, and a few months later the first franchise was received from Urbandale. The firm also acquired an existing cable operation in Creston that same year.

In 1972 three more cable systems were acquired and six more franchises were received. Heritage stock split two-for-one; a million-dollar public offering was complete; and the key franchise in the partners' early plans—Des Moines—came up for election.

Heritage won Des Moines and began construction in 1973. At the same time the Kansas City-Des Moines microwave route was completed. Over the next few years acquisitions and new franchise awards pushed Heritage into the top 50 cable television companies. Heritage was the second cable operator in the country to affiliate with Home Box Office, and new satellite-delivered movies on HBO were added to the Des Moines system in 1976.

In the late 1970s Heritage began diversifying by purchasing radio stations and display companies. A two-for-one stock split, completion of a $5-million public offering, and 28 new franchises set the stage for continued growth into the 1980s.

Heritage moved into the top 25 cable television companies in 1980, and that same year acquired major franchises in Mississippi, South Texas, and Iowa. Fifteen cable television systems were constructed that year.

In 1981 the rapid pace continued with a three-for-two stock split, a 10-percent dividend, and the completion of another public offering, this time for $16 million. The firm was listed on the New York Stock Exchange in May 1982, and the following year became the 15th-largest cable company in the country.

Continued growth in franchises and acquisitions, coupled with diversification into other communications areas, made Heritage an attractive buy for investors. Diversification included purchase of communication products companies that manufactured such items as projection screens, easels, lecterns, calendars, books, and trade show exhibits. Other diversification took the firm into television broadcast stations and outdoor advertising.

In 1985 the company took its biggest plunge in the industry by purchasing a troubled Dallas/Fort Worth cable franchise for $110 million. Such bold investments, coupled with a solid track record of sound fiscal management, began to attract acquisition-minded investment giants. The organization began to look at ways to avoid a hostile takeover.

In 1988 what was termed the largest business deal in Iowa history saw a group of top Heritage executives in concert with the nation's largest cable operator, Denver-based Tele-Communications Inc., offer $835 million for the firm. The leveraged buyout took Heritage out of public trading with ownership transferred from thousands of shareholders to the privately held new company.

Heritage Communications, Inc., has maintained its Des Moines headquarters and most of its top management since the merger. The company is now among the top 10 cable television operators nationally, serving more than one million subscribers in 300 communities in 18 states. The firm continues to operate some of its other non-cable enterprises as well.

JOHN DEERE DES MOINES WORKS

The sprawling complex of the John Deere Des Moines Works plant dominates this view looking to the southeast. The Des Moines Area Community College is upper right where the lake appears.

A Vermont blacksmith who had emigrated to Illinois turned his inventive mind to the problems of plowing the virgin prairie in the early nineteenth century. In 1837 he developed a plow that "scoured" or shed the sticky prairie earth. This invention marked the beginning of one of the largest producers of farm equipment in the world—Deere & Company.

The firm's growth is due in part to John Deere's philosophy. He began manufacturing products before he had firm orders, a common practice today, but an innovation in its time. Deere is also credited with establishing a dealer organization to stock his products in local communities. Such marketing encouraged farmers to vist the dealer and see the products firsthand.

The modern Deere & Company dates to 1911, when six noncompeting farm equipment companies and 22 selling organizations were brought together under one corporate umbrella. This established the company as a full-line manufacturer and distributor of farm equipment. In 1918, when American agriculture was beginning the shift from animal power to mechanical power, the firm acquired the Waterloo Gasoline Engine Company. At that time tractors became a part of the product line.

Since that first plow, Deere has grown into a diversified equipment manufacturer with products for the construction, logging, and lawn care industries, as well as its extensive line of agricultural implements.

The story of the John Deere facility in Des Moines is twofold. It began as a World War II ordnance factory that was used to manufacture small arms ammunition. The factory was built on 586 acres of land near Ankeny, north of Des Moines, at a cost of $53 million. At its peak the factory included 43 buildings and employed 19,000 workers, most of them women. During its short life, it produced nearly 4 billion cartridges.

The factory began a second phase when it was purchased by John Deere in 1947. The Des Moines Works started production with 546 employees, producing corn pickers and cultivators. Today it employs 1,300 with a multimillion-dollar annual payroll and produces 15 major product lines, including cotton-harvesting machines, tillage and seeding equipment.

The factory is best known for its cotton pickers—John Deere was the first company to produce the two-row and the four-row, self-propelled cotton pickers. Although the firm

PARTNERS IN PROGRESS

John Deere's first commercially successful cotton picker revolutionized the cotton industry in the South. The "old Number 8" proved itself as a sturdy machine that could pick clean.

had experimented with mechanical cotton picking as long ago as 1928, the Great Depression and World War II delayed actual production of the equipment. In 1950 the now-famous "Number 8" went into production and set cotton harvesting ahead several years.

On May 27, 1961, a special train left the Des Moines Works for Atlanta, Georgia. It was made up of 108 flatcars loaded with 441 John Deere cotton pickers worth $7 million. Described as "the single-largest shipment of farm machinery ever made by rail," the mile-long serpent of distinctive John Deere green and yellow marked the transition from predominately hand-harvested to predominately machine-harvested cotton in the South.

Another memorable day for the Des Moines Works was the visit in 1959 by Soviet Premier Nikita Khrushchev. A 35-car caravan carried the premier, his party, press, and security people to the factory for a tour.

The 1960s and early 1970s saw the factory expanding its line to include row-crop cultivators, field cultivators, corn head attachments, sugar beet harvesters, grain dryers, and rotary hoes. During this time the grain drill line was transferred from Horicon, Wisconsin, to Des Moines.

The successor to the Number 8 two-row cotton picker is this modern four-row unit—the 9950. John Deere is the largest manufacturer of cotton pickers in the world.

Design of equipment was centered around larger equipment, soil conservation, operator comfort, and convenience. Features such as cabs, power steering, and hydraulic folding equipment emerged. Tillage tools were developed to handle increasing amounts of surface residue and to reduce soil erosion. The factory also started developing combination tillage tools, which accomplished two or three tillage tasks in one pass to conserve fuel, manpower, and time.

In 1986 it was announced that design and marketing responsibility for tillage products produced at the Plow & Planter Works in Moline, Illinois, would be transferred to the Des Moines Works. This transfer included plows, disks, v-rippers, and roller harrows.

The 150th anniversary of Deere & Company and the 40th anniversary of the John Deere Des Moines Works were celebrated in 1987. To commemorate these events, the factory hosted an open house, and approximately 8,000 people toured the facility.

Today, in addition to the Des Moines Works, John Deere products are manufactured in more than 20 factories around the world. John Deere Des Moines Works products are marketed worldwide.

INTER-STATE ASSURANCE COMPANY

Above, R.E. Freeman explains a new product concept to a group of agents. He served the company as president from 1979 to 1988 and is now chairman of the board.

Prompt, courteous, and efficient service marked the opening of the Inter-State Business Men's Accident Association in April 1908. That year, less than three months after the company was formed, the first accident claim was paid—within four hours of company notification of the death.

Such prompt attention to clients' needs made the firm an immediate success. The founder, Ernest W. Brown, saw the need for a company that would provide income protection to business and professional men. Other organizations offered such protection, but it was costly. E.W. Brown's slogan became "Insurance at the cost to produce it."

The growth of the firm was swift, and a force of agents was hired to sell a changing array of products. Brown summed up Inter-State this way: "My goal is not to create a big company, but a best little one." Brown's "best little" company withstood even the tough financial times of the Depression. In order to continue to provide quality customer service and to avoid layoffs during those years, employees took a 50-percent cut in pay.

In 1931 the firm's name was changed to Inter-State Business Men's Accident Company.

E.W. Brown's son, Robert, was elected president of the firm in 1934. Like his father, he was dedicated to progressive client services. Among his innovations was the development of disability income policies for women (available as early as 1925).

In 1948 the company name was changed again, this time to the Inter-State Assurance Company, a name that reflected a broader product base. And in 1960 life insurance was added to the policy line.

Growth in assets, life insurance in force, and premium income highlighted the five years from 1965 to 1970, as Al A. Urban served the company as president.

The firm had been housed in the Brown Hotel at Fourth and Keosaqua until 1968. In November of that year it moved across the street to a remodeled building at 420 Keosaqua.

Philip A. Brown, grandson of the founder, assumed the presidency in 1970. During his tenure Inter-State became the first Iowa company to offer a Housewife's Disability Income Policy. His nine years as president also were marked by the development of other innovative insurance products.

A dramatic alteration in the insurance industry lay in the offing when in 1979 Robert E. Freeman, CLU, was named president. Guided by his leadership, Inter-State became the third U.S. company to introduce Universal Life insurance, in March 1980. Known as FLEX-LIFE, the new prod- uct helped to launch Inter-State into a growth pattern unprecedented in the company's history. That fall the firm introduced a new-term insurance policy featuring the industry's lowest-priced nonsmoker rates. In October 1981 FLEXLIFE II, a second-generation Universal Life policy, was introduced. And as the FLEXLIFE policies altered forever its company's way of doing business, Inter-State started planning the introduction of other interest-sensitive life insurance products.

The revolutionary products developed during the Freeman presidency positioned Inter-State on the forefront of the change and prompted field and home office personnel increases that led to the need to expand to larger quarters. In October 1983 the firm moved to 1206 Mulberry.

In May 1985 Inter-State became a wholly owned subsidiary of Central Life Assurance Company of Des Moines and was reorganized from a mutual to a stock life insurance company.

On June 7, 1988, Irish Life Assurance plc, Dublin, Republic of Ireland, through its U.S.-based subsidiary, Carrig International, Inc., became the new owner of Inter-State. Irish Life, one of Europe's largest insurance companies, has committed its resources and knowledge to Inter-State's expansion into new products, financial information, and solutions to meet the changing needs of its current and future policyholders.

This continued dedication to provide protection for today and security for tomorrow will be guided by the company's new president and chief executive officer Ronald M. Butkiewicz. Under this leadership, Inter-State will move into the future toward a new vision of product and services for all of its publics.

Inter-State Assurance's current office is located at 12th and Mulberry streets.

E.W. Brown, founder of Inter-State Assurance, is shown below in his office in the old Brown Hotel with his secretary around the time of World War I.

IOWA STATE BANK

George O'Dea, the founder of Iowa State Bank, had no plans for founding a financial empire. In the 1890s he; his father, Thomas; and brother Ed operated the O'Dea Hardware Company in the raucous railroad town of Valley Junction. By the turn of the century the family had returned their hardware business to the east side of Des Moines, where Thomas had operated the Entwistle & O'Dea Hardware Store as early as 1880.

A rough and enthusiastic man, O'Dea believed life was to be enjoyed to the fullest. He greatly enjoyed tinkering with machines. Using a truck chassis and a school bus shell, he made, for annual winter trips to St. Petersburg, a forerunner of the motor home, with its own generator and a 200-gallon water tank. One of his greatest joys was boating on the Mississippi River and in Minnesota, earning him the nickname "the Skipper."

The Skipper's various business ventures evolved from one another. He sold Maxwell autos out of his hardware store. Later he had dealerships for Durants, Fords and Lincolns, Hudsons, the Essex, the Star, and Chevrolets.

He sold the cars on time but found he lacked the cash within the auto company to carry the growing volume of car loans. O'Dea Finance Company was organized in the 1930s

Iowa State Bank as it appeared in the late 1950s.

George O'Dea, founder of the Iowa State Bank.

to fill this need. At its peak, O'Dea Finance Company had six branch offices statewide.

In 1940 George O'Dea announced to Hugh Gallagher, one of his most trusted employees, "Hugh, we're going to start a bank." The Skipper provided a needed service to the east side community and also controlled the cost of money for his finance company.

Iowa State Bank opened its doors at East Sixth and Locust on April 16, 1941. Capital reserves totaled $126,000, deposits $400,000. The original directors were George O'Dea, Hugh Gallagher, George Borg, A.E. Sargent, and William Broquist. George Frampton, a Nebraska banker, was president, but the guiding inspiration was the Skipper. Growth was immediate and dramatic. In just five years deposits increased to $6.1 million.

In 1950 Iowa State Bank built its headquarters facility at East Seventh and Locust. In 1956, when deposits passed the $14-million mark, a large addition more than doubled the size of the building.

O'Dea formed many other businesses—most have been sold, often to key employees. But Bankers Leasing Company has become one of the jewels of the O'Dea legacy. George O'Dea died on May 13, 1959, at the age of 80. He left complete control of the businesses to Hugh Gallagher and Elmer Burgeson: Burgeson was president of the leasing and finance company, and Gallagher was president of the bank.

The pair continued the traditions the Skipper established, and Iowa State Bank enjoyed continuous but conservative growth. In 1981 it truly merited its slogan of "Safe and Sound," for it was ranked as the 15th-strongest bank in America.

In 1986 Iowa State Bank Holding Company was created to better coordinate the activities of the bank and leasing company, allowing bank employees to include leasing options when developing a financing program for customers.

In 1987 Iowa State Bank deposits increased more than 7.7 percent over the preceding year. Total assets reached $107 million. A third branch office housing an expanded trust department opened downtown on the skywalk system.

Iowa State Bank's local ownership and commitment to serving the public remain as steady as when the Skipper was at the helm.

IOWA POWER

Iowa Power's new generating plant in the 1920s was built on the southeast side of Des Moines. Now in mothballs, the plant provided local power for many years and was expanded several times.

The meter readers were readily identifiable in their military-style uniforms in the 1920s. Today's service personnel are not dressed in such an intimidating fashion.

When the early traders and military personnel began living and working at the confluence of the Des Moines and Raccoon rivers, the idea of a public utility didn't exist. They met their needs through use of the materials around them. Wood provided a means of shelter and fuel for heat and cooking. Air conditioning was found where there was a breeze and some shade. Light in the evening hours came from a fire or tallow candles.

As settlers moved into the area and the community of Fort Des Moines began to grow, the population depended upon the same resources used by the earlier arrivals. Even when coal became a popular source of heat instead of wood, lighting was still dependent on candles or, in later years, oil.

In 1857 the Des Moines Gas Company was formed. About that time a gas-manufacturing works was built at Second and Elm. By 1865 some Des Moines streets were being lit by gas lamps.

In 1875 the Capital City Gas Light Company was organized and received a charter from the city in March 1876. The firm began a major project—installing gaslights throughout the downtown area. This was a major expansion of the limited gas lighting then in use. On the evening of November 23, 1876, the street lamps were lighted for the first time. There were about 1,000 of them, and each one had to be lighted separately.

In 1889 the company extended its service to the outlying towns of Greenwood, Capital Park, and North Des Moines. By this date it was furnishing gas for fuel purposes as well as for illumination. In 1906 the name was changed to the Des Moines Gas Company. Gas as a home fuel for lighting, cooking, and water heating made its first appearance in the form of coke gas, manufactured by coke ovens. By the turn of the century natural gas was being burned off in oil fields as a by-product of drilling, but it was impractical to pipe it long distances for home use. Without interstate pipelines, there was no way to market it to consumers.

In 1928 the Des Moines Electric Light Company purchased all the properties of the Des Moines Gas Company. In 1931 natural gas from Northern Natural Gas Company was being distributed in western Iowa, but in Des Moines it was first mixed with manufactured gas before distribution. It was not until after World War II that natural gas came into its own as a space heating fuel. In 1946 pure natural gas was being distributed in the Des Moines area.

When, in 1878, Thomas A. Edison invented the incandescent light bulb, the new technology heralded an era of dramatic change. Electricity was first furnished to Des Moines in 1878 by the Des Moines Edison Light, Heat, and Power Company. The little firm had meager equipment and a capitalization of only $10,000. Its plant was located at 113 Fifth Street near Vine. Only a small part of what is now downtown Des Moines was served by the company at first.

On January 1, 1886, there were just 396 electric meters in service. The total capacity of the little plant was about 300 kilowatt-hours. Less than 10 miles of power lines stretched throughout the Des Moines area. At rush times, when the most current was used, each bulb seemed little more than a glass

Newly installed street lighting is on display in this view of High Street in 1926. View is east from about 11th.

case with a feeble glowing wire inside. There were no electric streetlights, yet. In 1884 the firm, always a losing concern, was sold to the Des Moines Edison Light Company.

This new organization installed two small generators and provided electric service to a few customers in the immediate vicinity of the plant. Gradually, the plant was enlarged and more electric customers were served.

In the late 1800s a manager and bookkeeper took charge of the business office. Also employed were 2 linemen, 2 installers, and 12 others who worked as engineers and firemen in the powerhouse. By today's standards, working conditions were harsh.

Then there was no such thing as a weekend off for firemen, who were responsible for stoking the fire. They worked a full 12-hour day, seven days a week, at $1.25 per day. Sometimes they were paid cash, but at other times they accepted goods from local merchants unable to pay their utility bills.

It was not until 1900 that the Des Moines operation could show a profit.

In 1889 a new steam-generating plant was built on the river front north of Grand Avenue. At the same time service was extended to East Des Moines as far as East Seventh Street. Installers had considerable difficulty finding a way to string the power lines across the river. The problem was finally solved when the city allowed the company to run its wire beneath one of the bridges.

Several companies entered into competition with the General Edison Company, but none of them was able to compete for any length of time, and one by one they were taken over by the larger corporation.

In 1895 an important improvement was made in the kind of electric meter used. At that time the amount of electricity used by customers was measured by chemical meters. The meters utilized an electroplating device. After a 16-candlepower lamp had burned for 1,698 hours, one gram of zinc from a positive plate transferred to the negative plate of the meter.

The meter readers then removed the negative plates from meters and took them to the office to be weighed. This system, however, left much to be desired. For example, a fly landing on one side of the balance during weighing could increase a customer's monthly bill by 50 cents.

The new meters recorded watts, similar to those used today. The meter change allowed the firm to make its first major rate reduction: A flat fee of 15 cents per kilowatt-hour was charged. At about the same time people began to realize the advantages and usefulness of electricity around the home and office, and demand for service grew rapidly.

An early advertisement (below) touting the advantages of electricity from the Des Moines Electric Company.

Public Health and Public Safety
Are Assured Where
Des Moines Electric Company's Service is Used

In the Home our electric service is truly the "Servant in the House" giving perfect light, clear and odorless, and doing the washing, ironing, and sewing with great satisfaction to the housewife.

In the Street our electric service insures public safety through the use of over fourteen hundred arc and incandescent lamps, and more than three hundred fifty ornamental electroliers.

In the Store our electric service shows the goods in their true colors, and does not contaminate the air breathed by the clerks and customers.

In the Shop our eletric service drives the machines with great safety and convenience to the workmen.

Ours is a Public-be-pleased Policy

DES MOINES ELECTRIC COMPANY
Fifth and Mulberry Streets
Phones Walnut, 5300-5301-5302

The corporate name was modified from the Des Moines Edison Light Company to the Des Moines Electric Company in 1908, the Des Moines Railway and Light Company in 1909, and the Des Moines Electric Company in 1913.

In 1902 the network of wires on 35-foot poles in the business district was removed, and the wires were carried in underground conduits. A downtown plant was established on 10th Street in 1910, where alternating current could be changed into direct current for use in the business district. Several other substations were built in different parts of the city to extend service as the community grew.

Because demand for electricity increased dramatically around the turn of the century, the first steam turbogenerator was installed, rated at 4,000 kilowatts. In 1911 another generator was added, providing another 4,000 kilowatts.

Between 1915 and 1919 two more 4,000-kilowatt generators were added. The last addition to the old plant was made in 1921 with a 10,000-kilowatt unit. During this period boilers were also installed with these turbines so that in 1921 there were 18 boilers in the station. This original plant was eventually replaced by the River Hills Station, built in 1966.

Approximately 125 people were employed by the company in 1918. Linemen were often only temporary employees. About one-quarter were known as "Boomers"—men who came to Des Moines during the spring, carrying tools and looking for work. When asked if they were linemen, they boasted of the experience by saying, "I've clum some." When cold weather returned, the Boomers once again headed south.

The most common mode of transportation for meter readers serving industrial customers was a Model T roadster. Those who installed residential meters tied three or four on their backs and walked. If the company saw fit, they sometimes rode streetcars. Linemen had a small fleet of vehicles to choose from, including a 1912 Buick, a 1912 Locomobile, a 1912 Dart one-ton truck, and, interestingly enough, two electric trucks.

The company retired its horse and wagon used by the "pole gang" (men responsible for erecting power poles) in 1921 and acquired another truck. According to one veteran employee, the transition nearly caused a strike. The pole gang complained the new vehicle got them to the job "too quick."

In 1925 a 20,000-kilowatt generating plant was built southeast of Des Moines. Other units were added to the plant in 1926, 1938, 1949, 1950, 1954, and 1964. Now in mothballs, the facility stands ready for service if needed in the future.

Construction is under way in 1949 for Iowa Power and Light Company's new headquarters building at Ninth and Walnut.

Iowa Power's headquarters building in 1951 at Ninth and Walnut.

PARTNERS IN PROGRESS

Merle Hazen and Gale Hufford look at literature in the appliance showroom. Iowa Power sold electric appliances for many years.

Many noteworthy events occurred in the 1930s. As a result of the Depression, employees took a 20-percent cut in wages. Common laborers were hired for 35 cents an hour. Despite the difficult times, both the company and Iowa's capital city experienced tremendous growth. The population of Des Moines climbed to nearly 127,000, while the firm completed acquisition of 19 small utilities operating in an even greater number of towns.

In 1943 all of the properties were combined under the name Iowa Power and Light Company. By this time the firm had not only acquired the Des Moines Gas Company and the Des Moines Electric Light Company, but also the Iowa properties of Iowa-Nebraska Light and Power Company. The last major acquisition was the Council Bluffs territory in 1949.

Until 1950 Iowa Power and Light was itself controlled by Continental Gas and Electric, which was in turn a subsidiary of a large holding company, United Light and Railways.

Nearly 36 years after the formation of Iowa Power and Light Company, the corporate structure underwent another major change. In 1979 the organization became a subsidiary of Iowa Resources Inc., a holding company. Two years later electric, gas, and generation functions were separated into distinct operating divisions known as Iowa Power, Iowa Gas, and Iowa Generation. In January 1984 Iowa Gas Company became a wholly owned subsidiary of Iowa Resources and functioned as a sister company of Iowa Power and Light.

Then, in 1985, Iowa Gas Company was sold to Midwest Gas, putting the company completely out of the gas business for the first time in nearly 60 years. Today Iowa Power provides electric service to more than 100 communities in central and western Iowa.

The IPALCO office and showroom in Shenandoah during the early 1950s.

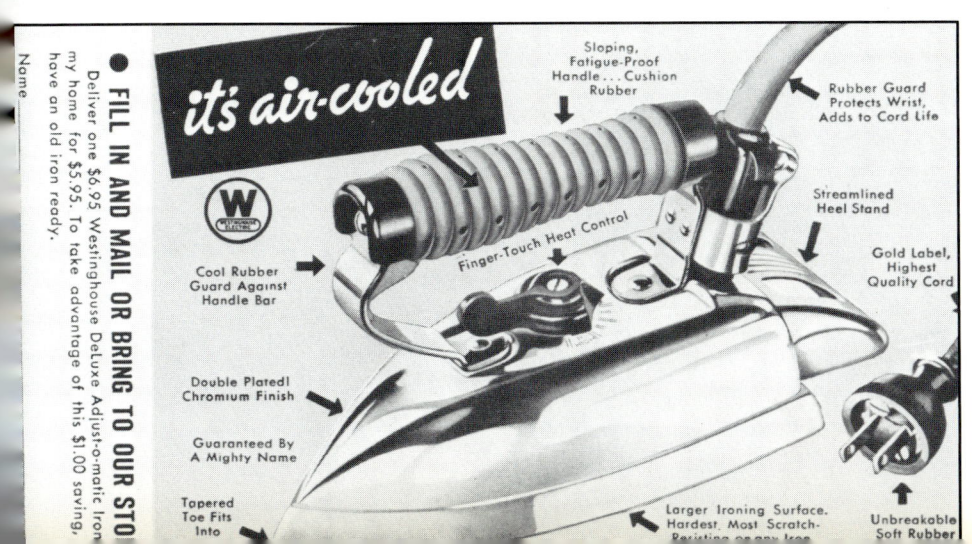

A promotional brochure distributed to Iowa Power and Light Company's customers offered this latest in electric irons for one dollar off its $6.95 price.

MERCY HOSPITAL MEDICAL CENTER DES MOINES

For 95 years Mercy Hospital Medical Center has celebrated many of Iowa's medical firsts: the oldest continuously operating hospital in Des Moines, the first isotope laboratory in Polk County, and the first heart transplant in central Iowa.

But among the fanfare surrounding Mercy's medical landmarks has been a quiet recognition of the smaller, daily miracles at the hospital: the birth of a baby, the progress of a cancer patient, or the first steps of a stroke victim.

It is with this pairing of dedication to medical advancement and devotion to compassion that Mercy has been a prominent fixture in Des Moines' history and now stands on the threshold of its second century.

In 1893 Des Moines' population of 52,000 was growing quickly. On December 8 of that year Mercy Hospital opened its doors at Hoyt Sherman Place on Woodland Avenue. The hospital had two private rooms and a ward for five patients. Patients were charged between $2.50 and six dollars per day with an additional fee of two dollars to five dollars for surgery.

A group of Sisters of Mercy gathers to look over the site as construction of Mercy's South Wing gets under way.

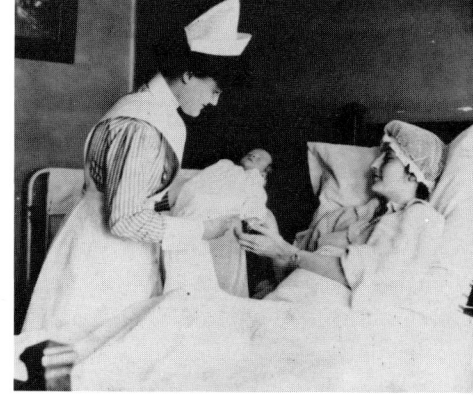

A maternity ward nurse presents a newborn baby to the mother in 1915.

From this modest start by six nuns has evolved a $95-million, 535-bed medical center with more than 2,500 employees. Mercy was started by the Sisters of Mercy, an order founded by Catherine McAuley in Dublin, Ireland, in 1831. Sixteen years later the Sisters established the first hospital in the United States and, by the 1890s, had founded more than 30 hospitals in this country, including Mercy Hospital in Des Moines.

Mercy's roots trace back to a pioneer priest, the Reverend John Brazill, who came to Des Moines in 1860. He recognized the need for a hospital and, in 1876, appointed the first hospital board of trustees. Upon his death he left a trust to establish a Catholic hospital. His successor, Monsignor Michael Flavin of St. Ambrose Church, asked the Most Reverend Henry Cosgrove, bishop of Davenport, to send some Sisters of Mercy to establish a hospital.

Soon after, the six nuns arrived and began operations at Hoyt Sherman Place. A total of 221 patients were served that first year.

In 1895 the hospital dedicated its first permanent building at Fourth and Ascension streets on the site of the present campus. The East Wing, as it was known, was four stories, cost $50,000, and had room for 12 patients. It included a convent, chapel, and nurses' quarters.

In 1897 the Central Wing was built, and two other additions were built in 1908 and 1912. During the early 1900s the hospital operated a clinic for Drake Medical School students, opened the Mercy School of Nursing, and began a training program for interns and residents.

By the 1930s Mercy could boast of its pathological laboratory; its X-ray, pediatrics, and orthopedic departments; and its electrocardiograph machine, and by the 1940s the hospital had roughly 220 beds.

Drake University medical students observe an operation in Mercy's surgery amphitheater in the early 1900s.

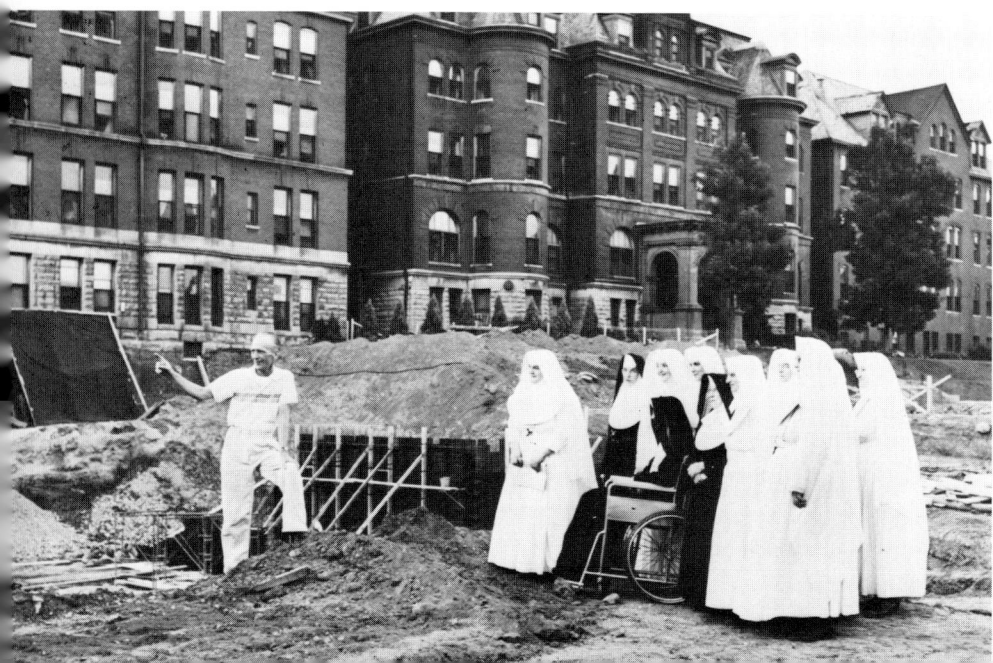

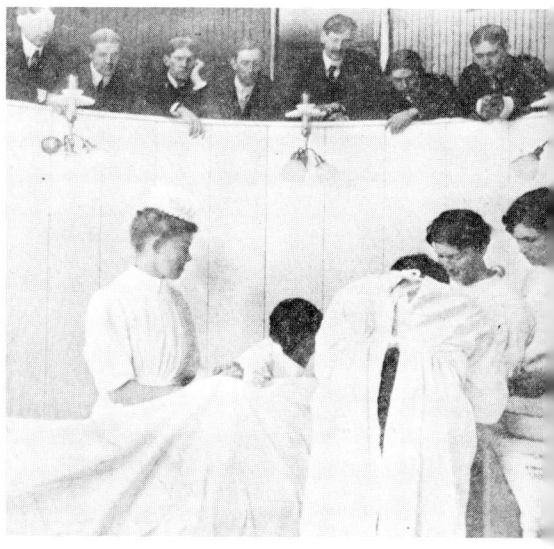

By 1935 Mercy was offering physicians' clinics, a forerunner of today's Medical Education Department, on a regular basis. One clinic that year featured 41 surgeries, including a rare surgery to promote fertility in a 30-year-old woman.

The hospital did not escape the turmoil wrought by World War II. At one point 29 Mercy doctors and 51 School of Nursing alumnae were in the service. Shortages of supplies were a constant worry. Nurses recall having to save on gauze by tearing it into smaller pieces and recycling it by resterilizing when possible. Mercy and two other Des Moines hospitals offered a training program for the U.S. Cadet Nurse Corps, which offered incentives to women entering the nursing profession.

But the war also brought enormous medical progress. Doctors returned from the war with new procedures for treating serious injuries and burns, plus a greater knowledge of plastic surgery. Penicillin, the "wonder drug," was introduced, followed quickly by cortisone and important tranquilizers.

Steady growth continued with a new School of Nursing building in 1946. Seven years later Mercy was the first hospital in Des Moines to install an isotope laboratory to treat cancer.

The late 1940s brought administrative changes as well. Administrator Sister Mary Anita Paul had long had a dream of establishing an advisory board composed of people not directly connected with the hospital. A group of civic leaders had been instrumental in raising funds for the new nursing school home, and in early 1947 Sister Mary Anita invited them to sit on the first hospital advisory board.

The first board members were Bishop Gerald Bergan, John Brooks, the Reverend Raymond Conley, Edwin Buckley, Charles Gifford, A.T. Gormley, Harold Klein, E.H. Mullock, Morey Sostrin, Mrs. J.J. Kelly, Mrs. John Normile, and Mrs. Maurice Northrup. For more than 40 years the advisory boards and other boards have provided valuable service and advice to Mercy administrators.

Not long after the advisory board was formed, the Mercy Hospital Guild was created to unite the women of Des Moines and instill interest in the hospital and its School of Nursing. In fewer than six months the guild grew

–*Mercy Hospital Medical Center at night—1987.*

On December 1, 1986, the first kidney transplant at Mercy was performed on Andrew Peitzman of Ames. Shown (below) are transplant surgeon Dr. Cass Franklin (left), Dr. Guy Stines (center), and surgery nurse Jane Krogmann.

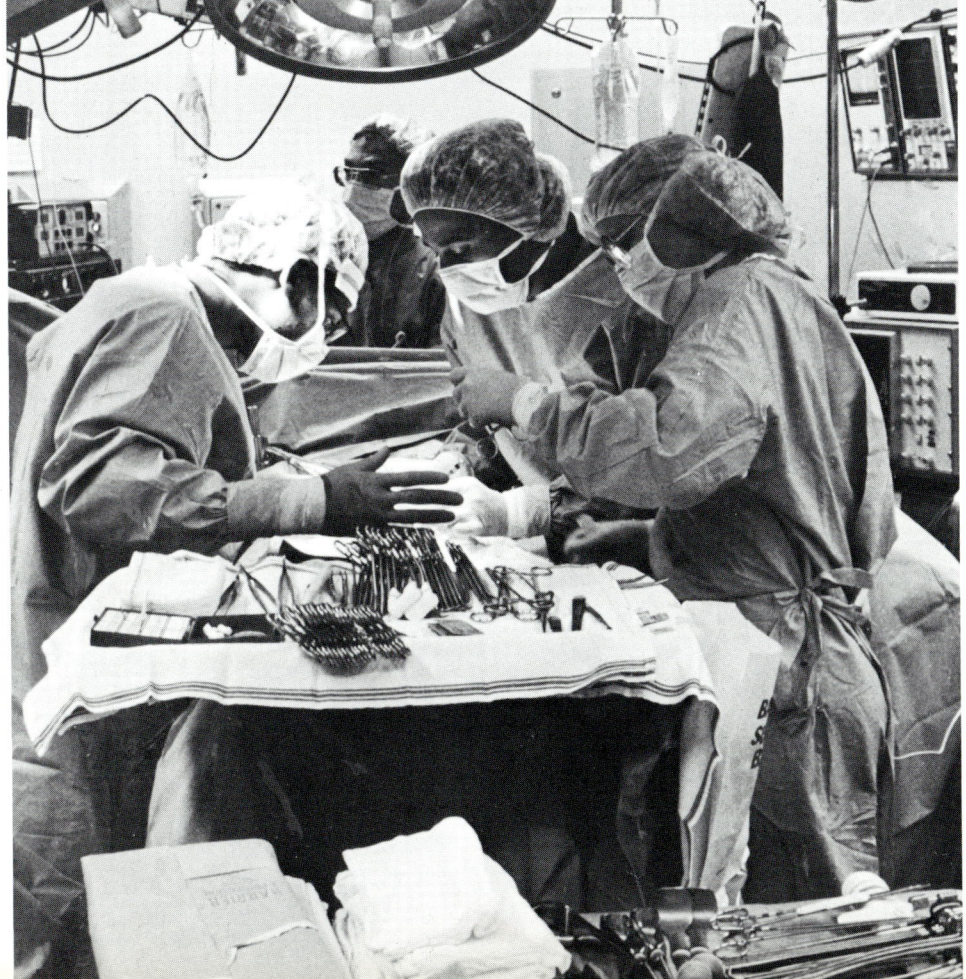

Mercy has gained an enviable reputation as a heart transplant center. Two of those transplant patients, Richard Kelley and David Maland, visit while undergoing therapy.

to more than 200 members. Today its membership of approximately 775 provides an average of $80,000 annually to support the hospital.

In 1951 Mercy treated 11,179 patients, and 1,853 babies were born in its maternity ward. The overall occupancy rate of the hospital was 95 percent. In 1955 the Sisters of Mercy announced plans for a South Wing to add 108 beds. The wing was completed in 1959, after $2.4 million had been raised. The hospital now had 361 beds.

If the 1950s were characterized by steady growth, the 1960s and 1970s were marked by a multimillion-dollar expansion to keep up with the demand for more sophisticated medical services. Buildings added to the Mercy campus during this period included a convent, chapel, intern apartments, and a 10-story, H-shaped tower that brought the total number of beds to 500.

A typical year sees more than 25,000 patients admitted, more than 2,600 babies born, and more than 18,000 surgical procedures performed. The new hospital became fully utilized so quickly that the need for expansion soon became apparent.

In the 1980s Mercy purchased the former Americana Apartments, Quality Health Care Center, the former General Growth Building, the former Howard Johnson Motel, the Mid-Town Motor Inn, the Bethel Mission site, the former Bishop Drumm Home, Charlie's Showplace, and a former convenience store at the corner of Sixth and University avenues.

The buildings are used for offices, apartments for the elderly, the School of Nursing, the Willis Adult and Respite Care Center, and the House of Mercy for low-income women and their children.

Other additions to the campus include a four-story heart institute, a cancer center, two other medical office buildings, an activity center for senior citizens, and parking ramps to handle 1,200 vehicles. Mercy opened its first Mercy Medical Clinic at Valley West Mall in 1983, and since has opened 10 other clinics in the Des Moines area.

Cardiac care has been one of Mercy's important care areas for many years. In 1905 a stabbing victim was having his chest wound packed with gauze when his heart stopped. Dr. W.S. Conkling reached into the wound, massaged the heart, and it started again. The victim recovered, and the incident aroused great curiosity in medical circles. It was written up in the *New York Medical Journal.*

In 1953 Mercy became only the fourth hospital in the country to receive funds from the American Heart Association for a program to evaluate heart patients and determine the degree of work they could tolerate. Mercy's first coronary care unit was opened in 1968, and three years later Mercy began offering coronary angiograms and open-heart surgery. Since the cardiac catheterization laboratory opened in 1976, it has become the busiest in the state, with more than 4,500 cardiac procedures each year.

The progress in cardiac technology at Mercy reached new heights July 6, 1985, when heart surgeons transplanted the heart of an accident victim into the chest of Paul Sarnecki. It was the first heart transplant in central Iowa. Since then there have been more than 25 such transplants. In addition, the hospital performs kidney and cornea transplants, and is beginning heart/lung and lung transplants—one of 10 such centers in the nation doing these operations.

The growing emphasis in medical circles on prevention, wellness, and in-home care has led to expanded services from Mercy. The hospital sponsors programs on nutrition, heart attack prevention, pain, fitness, weight loss, sleep disorders, and quitting smoking. Also offered are emotional support groups and 24-hour hot lines for those wanting information on cancer, coronary care, substance abuse, and burns. Mercy also provides alcohol and drug recovery programs, has been a leader in geriatric services, and has reached out to assist rural hospitals with medical and managerial expertise.

Mercy's emergency department treats more than 40,000 patients each year, making it the busiest in the state. In addition, Mercy's Air Life emergency medical helicopter can be anywhere in Iowa in less than one hour.

In almost 100 years Mercy Hospital Medical Center has grown to be one of Iowa's premier medical centers. Its mission today, under president Sister Patricia Clare Sullivan, remains to provide compassionate care, to never overlook the needs of a patient or family member, and to never overlook the small miracles.

KIRKE-VAN ORSDEL, INCORPORATED

Kirke-Van Orsdel, Incorporated, headquartered in downtown Des Moines' Capital Square, is one of the largest and fastest-growing privately owned companies in the United States.

Now a conglomerate of six major divisions, the firm has grown from a staff of two to more than 800 employees with offices located in Des Moines, Iowa; Chicago, Illinois; New York, New York; Washington, D.C.; Columbia, South Carolina; Richmond, Virginia; Tampa, Florida; and London, England.

Clients include the nation's most influential associations: the National Rifle Association (NRA), The Retired Officers Association (TROA), Reserve Officers Association (ROA), American Institute of Architects (AIA), American Society for Travel Agents (ASTA), Texas Society of Certified Public Accountants (TSCPA), National Guard Association of the United States (NGAUS), and Massachusetts Medical Society (MMS), to mention a few—a very impressive multimillion-dollar track record for a company just 14 years young!

Working on an uncanny insight of the lucrative potential for growth in the association insurance business, Des Moines natives and high school buddies Gerald M. Kirke and William A. Van Orsdel teamed forces in 1974 to form Kirke-Van Orsdel, Incorporated (KVI), a full-service insurance broker-administrator of group insurance plans for national associations.

In the beginning KVI operated on a shoestring budget. Kirke and Van Orsdel were the only employees, and spent their days living out of suitcases and knocking on doors in a scramble to line up potential customers. An answering machine handled business at the "home office."

Drive, hard work, and professional expertise paid off in 1976 when the Reserve Officers Association became Kirke and Van Orsdel's first major client.

Two years later, despite competition from 40 other brokerage houses, KVI won the opportunity to prepare and administer a unique property/casualty insurance plan for the then 900,000 (now nearly 3 million) members of the National Rifle Association. In 1980 KVI put together the second-largest group insurance program in the country for The Retired Officers Association.

KVI was up and running!

And in the years to follow Kirke-Van Orsdel, Incorporated, was to experience a phenomenal pattern of growth—and change. Today the firm has expanded well beyond the boundaries of the insurance brokerage field and now operates six major divisions worldwide:

Kirke-Van Orsdel Association Division—a full-service broker/administrator specializing in the design and administration of membership services for national associations.

Kirke-Van Orsdel Insurance Services—offers full-service insurance broker services including the design and administration of personal, commercial, and group insurance programs.

The founders of Kirke-Van Orsdel, Incorporated (from left), Gerald M. Kirke and William A. Van Orsdel.

The KVI Center on Third Street north of downtown Des Moines.

Kirke-Van Orsdel Management Corporation—an independent company created to assist high-risk industries develop risk-retention groups, essentially private insurance companies solely devoted to providing liability coverage to its members.

Johnson & Higgins/Kirke-Van Orsdel, Inc.—a joint venture with the biggest privately held insurance broker in the world. J&H/KVI specializes in the development of mass-merchandised insurance products for clients who represent a major share of the *Fortune* 1,000 largest corporations in America.

Kirke-Van Orsdel Group Administrators—serves the group insurance administration needs of national trade and professional associations.

Willis Faber/Kirke-Van Orsdel—a partnership with Willis Faber, a large London-based insurance firm providing services to unique and growing worldwide markets.

Throughout its rapid growth and development, Kirke-Van Orsdel, Incorporated, has found it advantageous to maintain corporate headquarters in Des Moines. The city is the second-largest insurance center in the nation, has one of the nation's largest concentration of printing plants, and is also the home of one of the largest bulk mail centers in the country.

And, according to Van Orsdel, there is one other reason the company will remain in the Midwest. "When we make sales calls, we find people trust people from Iowa," he says.

That makes sense. After all, it was Iowans who made Kirke-Van Orsdel, Incorporated, what it is today.

POLK COUNTY

RUAN CORPORATION

The Ruan story is an Iowa story. It begins in the middle of the Depression.

The year was 1932. John Ruan had just completed a year at Iowa State University in Ames. His father, a physician in Beacon, Iowa, had recently died, leaving the family with two automobiles and little else. A classmate at Iowa State suggested that Ruan trade one of the cars for a truck and haul gravel for a local road builder to earn some money during the summer. Less than a year later Ruan had a fleet of three units hauling coal.

"We each made three round trips a day," Ruan recalls. "Each truck could handle seven tons, and you shoveled it on and you shoveled it off—42 tons a day. I made muscles and I made money at the same time.

"I created three direct jobs, plus several indirect jobs at the mine, and I saved my customers 50 cents per ton over the prevailing price. Further, we had dividers in the truck boxes so we could deliver as little as a half-ton, if that was all the customer could afford. That was service, and we've been an innovator in services through all the intervening years."

It was this early work ethic—this dedication to customer service—that created a spirit, the Ruan Spirit, which led to the development of what is now the largest privately owned transportation company in the country.

The beginning of the Ruan Companies was in trucking, and John Ruan is one of trucking's true pioneers. His early ingenuity led to a long series of achievements that have earned Ruan national recognition as the leader in innovative transportation engineering and safety.

Headquartered in Des Moines, Ruan Transportation Management Systems employs 3,000 people and operates more than 170 facilities nationwide. In a single year Ruan will furnish customers with more than 13,000 vehicles operating over 750 million miles annually.

From full-service leasing to contract carriage and a national rental fleet, Ruan provides a complete range of transportation alternatives to the national markets. In the local market, Ruan owns and operates the Avis car rental franchise and the Des Moines taxicab companies.

The first significant move toward diversification within the Ruan Companies came in 1964, when John Ruan acquired Bankers Trust Company, an independent bank established in 1917 with headquarters in Des Moines.

Since the bank was acquired, it has grown to become one of the largest commercial banks in Iowa. Long a supporter of local entrepreneurs, the bank has played an important role in launching some of the most successful companies in the state.

While Bankers Trust continued to grow and develop a strong franchise within the state of Iowa, Ruan realized that the needs of its customers would become more and more involved with the international marketplace. In anticipation of those needs, the bank put in place an international banking department with more than 100 banking relationships in 70 countries.

Ruan continued to pursue his vision of expanding international opportunities, and in 1983 formed the Iowa Export-Import Trading Company, which now does business in 35 countries and serves more than 400 domestic and international customers. Several of Iowa's largest corporations joined Ruan as shareholders in this venture.

The trading company has offices in several foreign countries and has ex-

Ruan Cab Company provided free transportation to a camp at Grandview Park in 1949 for the Polk County Society for the Crippled and Disabled.

John Ruan with two of his grandchildren, John Ruan IV (left) and Jonathan Ruan Fletcher (right), in 1974 when the 36-story building bearing his name was already dominating the Des Moines skyline.

One of Ruan Transport's MEGAFLEET units.

tended its overseas presence through the Ruan membership in the World Trade Center Association, which provides locations in more than 50 nations.

Ruan also anticipated continued expansion within the financial service industry. That led to a decision by the Ruan Companies in 1985 to establish Ruan Securities Corporation, an independent full-service brokerage operation with national headquarters in Des Moines and a regional office in West Palm Beach, Florida.

Throughout the many years of growth within the Ruan Companies, John Ruan has always remained loyal to Iowa and to Des Moines. It was this loyalty that caused Ruan to choose Des Moines as the site for development of the Ruan international headquarters. This decision by Ruan was to strike a new beginning for downtown Des Moines.

In the early 1970s, as downtown Des Moines was showing signs of decay, John Ruan purchased several old buildings and demolished them to build the 36-story Ruan Center, which for many years has been the state's largest office building. Soon after the completion of that project, Ruan provided the leadership as general partner with a group of local investors to build the 34-story Marriott Hotel next to the Ruan Center.

Ruan also was responsible for skywalk connections between the Ruan Center and an adjacent parking garage. A subsequent skywalk connected the Ruan Center with the Marriott Hotel. These early skywalk developments were the first of what would become an extensive downtown skywalk system connecting almost all office buildings, public buildings, and parking facilities. A subsequent addition to the Ruan Center complex was the 14-story Two Ruan Center.

This personal effort and community leadership by John Ruan led to the revitalization of downtown Des Moines, which ultimately provided motivation for development throughout the entire state.

Recognition followed. In 1981 Ruan was named Des Moines' Citizen of the Year, and the following year he was elected to the Iowa Business Hall of Fame.

John Ruan has used this same level of personal energy and commitment in support of numerous charities. The most significant personal effort was in 1975, when he established the John Ruan MS/Charity. It is one of the nation's largest activities to provide funds for the fight against multiple sclerosis.

In 1985 he was given the distinguished Iowa Citizen Award by the Mid-Iowa Council of Boy Scouts of America, and the following year he was given the Humanitarian Award by the Variety Club of Iowa. That same year he was honored by the Iowa Society to Prevent Blindness with its annual People With Vision Award. This award is presented each year to an outstanding person with a clear perspective and farsightedness in community service, and devotion to fellow citizens throughout the state.

Perhaps the citation in that one award best typifies the man—for John Ruan is truly a man of vision, who has always been willing to commit his personal time, effort, and money as an investment in the future, and that personal investment—an extension of the Ruan Spirit—has benefited not only his companies, but also the community he calls home: Des Moines, Polk County, and the entire state of Iowa.

John Ruan accepts an Award of Merit for his company's safety record at a meeting of the National Tank Truck Carriers, Inc., in 1950.

DRAKE UNIVERSITY

Confronted with declining economic conditions after two decades of apparent prosperity, The Disciples of Christ in Iowa were faced with the decision to move their established Oskaloosa College, the first Christian college founded in Iowa, to another location.

In 1881 a group led by George Carpenter journeyed to Des Moines, where it found individuals ready to support the proposed move. In March 1881, bolstered with a $20,000 pledge from General Francis Marion Drake of Centerville, for whom the university was named, the new educational institution became a reality.

This was Drake University's modest beginning. Carpenter served as Drake's first president and chancellor from 1881 to 1893. During his tenure the university established itself as an integral part of the young Iowa capital city. In 10 years it boasted eight departments, 53 teachers, and more than 800 students.

In 1888 a university plan was developed that separated the departments

This symbolic ground breaking in the spring of 1986 marked the start of a massive renovation and construction program in the Drake area. From the left are Drake president Michael Ferrari, developer Bill Knapp, U.S. Congressman Neal Smith, and Hawkeye Bank president J. Michael Earley.

from colleges. The early colleges included the College of Letters and Science, the Normal College, the Music College, the Business College, and the Bible College.

Upon the death of president Carpenter, Barton O. Aylesworth was named acting chancellor and president and served until 1897, when William Bayard Craig assumed the role of chancellor.

As demands for more specialized education were received from the business and professional communities, Drake expanded its academic programs and established new ones as they were needed. Much of this growth took place at the turn of the century during the administration of president Hill M. Bell (1902 to 1918).

One of the greatest educators and administrators that Drake and the state of Iowa has ever had, Bell led

The Students' Home was the first building on the present-day site of Drake University. It housed students, offices, and classrooms. It was razed after a few years.

Drake through a major building program and the economic difficulties that began with the outbreak of World War I in 1914. So successful were his efforts that he was elected president of the Association of American Colleges in 1917-1918. During his administration Cole Hall, which now houses the Admissions Office, was built in 1904 as the home for the Law School. The following year Memorial Hall, now home for the Graduate School of Education, was completed for the Bible College. An addition to Howard Hall was completed in 1908-1909, and Carnegie Hall was erected in 1907.

The year 1893 marked the advent of organized, planned sports at Drake. The coming of John L. Griffith as coach and director of athletics in 1908 accelerated the growth of the sports program. The "D" Club was organized that year. Under Coach Griffith, the Drake teams, which had variously been called Ducklings, Drakes, Ganders, and even Tigers, became the Bulldogs. However, Griffith's greatest contribution to the university was made in 1910, when he organized America's great track and field classic, the Drake Relays.

Old Main, the university's first permanent building, is a Des Moines landmark. Built in 1882, it currently houses administrative offices.

Drake's fifth president, Arthur Holmes (1918-1922), turned to peacetime planning following the war. He set up a psychological clinic, established the Department of Physical Education, and set up an elementary school as a practice school for prospective teachers.

In 1922 Daniel W. Morehouse (1922-1941) began his tenure as president. Morehouse, an astronomer, was recognized for the discovery of a comet that bears his name. The City of Des Moines built an observatory at Waveland Golf Course for his use. During this period a Phi Beta Kappa chapter was established, and new student residences and classroom facilities were built. In 1937 the Gardner Cowles Foundation donated funds for Cowles Library, and in 1966 the foundation underwrote an addition to the original building that tripled its size.

Following Morehouse's death in 1941, the responsibility for leading the university through the chaotic period of World War II fell to the administration of Henry G. Harmon (1941-1964). Harmon's administration established the office of Dean of Students in 1945 and a community college the following year. Between 1946 and 1966, sixteen new buildings designed by distinguished architects Eliel and Eero Saarinen, Ludwig Mies van der Rohe, Harry Weese and Associates, and Brooks, Borg and Skiles were constructed on the campus. The variety of architectural styles has brought national attention to the campus.

Under the leadership of president Paul F. Sharp, the period from 1966 to 1971 was characterized by rapid growth and development. Library resources increased by more than 50 percent, and the size and quality of the faculty increased. To support the developments, a capital campaign, the Centennial Development Program, was launched.

In 1972 Dr. Wilbur C. Miller was named president. During his tenure several important buildings were completed as a part of the Centennial Development Program, including the Harmon Fine Arts Center in 1972, the Olmsted Center in 1974, the Olin Hall of Biological Science in 1975, the Law School's Cartwright Hall in 1976, the Bell Center for Physical Education and Recreation in 1977, and Aliber Hall (College of Business and Public Administration) in 1982. In the midst of these developments, Drake University celebrated its centennial in 1981.

In 1985 Dr. Michael R. Ferrari became president. President Ferrari guided a major reorganization of the university's academic and administrative structures and led efforts that resulted in a new governing board. An Honors Program and new nursing programs were initiated as well.

The decline in the business district and neighborhood adjacent to the university led to the creation of a Drake Neighborhood Association and the Drake/Des Moines Development Corporation. Improvements in the neighborhood have been apparent, and new construction in the business district has added a motel, three apartment complexes, the Drake Law School Legal Clinic building, and a new restaurant—The Drake Diner.

The university has moved into the age of high technology with a campus-wide computer-enriched curriculum program and a new, state-of-the-art telecommunications system.

The Drake Relays, begun in 1910, has become one of the premier track and field carnivals in the nation. The relays attracts thousands to Des Moines every spring.

EQUITABLE OF IOWA COMPANIES

Equitable of Iowa's home office in 1893.

Iowa was young, barely 20 years old, and stagecoaches still provided much of the transportation to the capital city of Des Moines, when 16 men gathered in the law office of Judge Phineas Casady in January 1867 to plan the formation of an insurance company. They had been called together by Frederick M. Hubbell, a 28-year-old lawyer and the youngest member of the group.

He believed an Iowa-based company could profit by providing insurance services to the people of the state and keeping the funds within the state.

The company was organized January 25, 1867, with Hubbell insisting that Judge Casady be president. Casady had been the first to settle in Des Moines and had given Hubbell his first job when the young man had arrived with his father at age 16 in 1855. Casady is also credited with naming the new company, supposedly after the revered Equitable of London.

Thus was born one of Iowa's oldest businesses, the first insurance company founded west of the Mississippi River.

Wesley Redhead, a coal mine operator, was named vice-president; Hubbell was elected secretary; B.F. Allen, who at 38 had already amassed a fortune, was chosen treasurer; and Hoyt Sherman, banker, lawyer, and former postmaster, was named actuary.

It was Allen, a banker and Iowa's first millionaire, who built Terrace Hill for $250,000 in 1867. Allen lost his fortune following the depression of 1873, primarily through the failure of a Chicago bank he had purchased a few years earlier. Hubbell bought Terrace Hill at a reduced price in 1884, after it had been on the market for 10 years. Terrace Hill is now the Iowa governor's home.

Hubbell bought the company's first policy in the amount of $2,000. A year later, with fewer than 1,000 policyholders, the firm had $427,000 of insurance in force and assets of $126,946. Now, more than 120 years later, Equitable has more than $6 billion of life insurance in force and does business in 38 states.

The Equitable's first offices were on the second floor of the Hoyt Sherman Block at the northeast corner of Court Avenue and Third Street. Judge Casady remained president until 1871. He was succeeded by Allen in 1872 and 1873, who was followed by Hoyt Sherman, who served from 1874 to 1887. Hubbell became president in 1888 and served in that capacity until he was elected chairman of the board in 1907.

Almost from the beginning Hubbell bought all of the Equitable stock he could. He bought out Jefferson Polk in 1888, and by 1896 Hoyt Sherman's name was also absent from the list of stockholders.

Cyrus Kirk succeeded Hubbell as president in 1907 and served for the next five years, until James C. Cummins assumed the position. He was followed in 1919 by Hubbell's eldest son, Frederick Cooper Hubbell. By then the insurance in force was $160 million, and assets surpassed $25 million. F.C. Hubbell did not want to direct the company, but illness forced Cummins to resign and F.M. Hubbell insisted his son take the position. After two years he was succeeded by Henry S. Nollen, who served as president until 1939.

Land was acquired at the southwest corner of Sixth and Locust streets in downtown Des Moines as the site for a new home office. On June 1, 1924, the 319-foot, 19-story structure was completed. It was the tallest building west of the Mississippi, and for years was Iowa's tallest building.

Through the years the firm continued to grow and prosper. In 1977 a new holding company, Equitable of Iowa Companies, was formed with Equitable Life Insurance Company, E.I. Sales, Inc., and Equitable Investment Services, Inc., as wholly owned subsidiaries. Two years later the Des Moines-based Younkers department store chain was purchased by the Equitable of Iowa Companies.

The Equitable Building was under construction for two years and was completed in 1924. It remained Iowa's tallest building for nearly 50 years. This view looks east on Locust.

YOUNKERS, INC.

Younkers traces its origins back to 1856, when Samuel, Lipman, and Marcus Younkers, three brothers from Poland, founded a small dry-goods store in Keokuk. Keokuk was, at that time, a bustling river town and the gateway to central Iowa. Although Younkers prospered, the brothers could see the decline in river traffic and the need to move west with the population.

In 1874 they sent a younger stepbrother, Herman, to Des Moines with $6,000 to establish their first branch store. This farsighted move placed the business in the heart of Iowa's largest city and established Des Moines as the center of Younkers' new operation with the closing of the Keokuk store in 1879.

Younkers had always been a pioneer in innovative retail practices. In 1881, following this tradition, Younkers became the first store in Des Moines to employ a woman, Mary McCann, as a sales associate. Business was then believed to be a man's world, but McCann soon proved her worth as female customers sought her out, enjoying the idea of being served by another woman.

At the turn of the century Younkers was earning the reputation of a well-respected home store chain. Although prosperous and well-managed, Younkers cautiously began to expand its store operations. By early 1909 the store expanded its five-story location at the corner of Seventh and Walnut to a seven-story building. Expansion again took place in the 1920s, when a series of mergers established

Younkers moved to its current downtown location in 1900. The store today looks much as it did from the outside in the 1930s, when this view was made. Over the past few years the exterior has been restored, while the interior has been extensively remodeled.

Younkers as the dominant department store in Des Moines.

In 1923 Younkers began to expand the downtown store by acquiring Wilkins Department Store, and later acquiring Younkers' two major rivals—J. Mandelbaum and Sons and Harris Emery stores.

Younkers successfully weathered the Depression of the 1930s as well as World War II and began a phase of expansion that would establish it as the dominant retailer in Iowa. In 1941 the first branch store was opened in Ames, and before the end of the decade Younkers opened branches in Mason City, Fort Dodge, Sioux City, Marshalltown, and Iowa City.

In 1948, due to the successful nature of the retail business, Younkers offered the sale of its stock to the public. Expansion continued in the 1950s with stores built in Ottumwa and in the three states contiguous to Iowa: Omaha, Nebraska; Moline, Illinois; and Austin, Minnesota. The first store in a shopping center was also opened in 1955 at The Center in Omaha, Nebraska. The chain continued to expand into two Des Moines shopping malls in the late 1950s, with the opening of stores at Merle Hay Mall and Eastgate in 1962.

By the mid-1970s the chain had expanded into five states with some 26 Younkers' stores. In 1979 Equitable of Iowa Companies acquired Younkers, Inc., by merger. New management was recruited, and a number of changes were made. The new executive committee, made up of savvy retailers from all over the United States, led Younkers to profitability and dominance in the state of Iowa.

In 1986 a new distribution center was built in Ankeny, replacing the two former locations in Davenport and Omaha. In 1987 Younkers, Inc., on behalf of Equitable of Iowa Companies, made an offer to purchase all 11 Brandeis department stores located throughout Nebraska and Iowa. This acquisition established Younkers, now made up of some 5,000 associates, as the 40th-largest retailer in the nation and brought the chain to some 37 stores spanning five contiguous states.

The future of Younkers, Inc., echoes its past as the company has been and continues to be devoted to the policy of Satisfaction Always.

The Younkers executive committee (from left): Robert Ferguson, vice-president/marketing and sales promotion; Sidney Pearlman, vice-president/general merchandise manager; Jack Prouty, vice-president/chief financial officer; Gerry Roth, executive vice-president; Tom Gould, president and chief executive officer; Don Cato, vice-president/operations; Bob Mosco, vice-president/general merchandise manager; David Sanguinetti, vice-president of stores; and George Christopher, vice-president/general merchandise manager. Not pictured is Chuck Nelson, vice-president/human resources.

NEUMANN BROTHERS, INC.

Neumann Brothers, Inc., has given Des Moines its skyline—starting in 1924 with the state's first "skyscraper," the 19-story Equitable Building, to the 36-story Ruan Center, the Marriott Hotel, American Republic Insurance Company, and the domed Botanical Center.

Looking northeast across Grand Avenue as construction begins on the Insurance Exchange Building in 1922. Note the horse-drawn wagons hauling the dirt from the excavation.

The firm was started in 1912, when at the age of 28, Arthur H. Neumann began A.H. Neumann Company. The firm's first contract was for a dormitory for the Des Moines College, then located at 10th Street and College Avenue. Known as Childs Hall, it was to be the first major commission in a long line of projects completed by his company.

After his brothers Walter, Oscar, and Harold completed their college training, each in a special engineering line, they came to work for the firm, and in 1932 the organization was renamed Arthur H. Neumann and Brothers, a name retained until 1976.

When the sons of the four principal Neumann Brothers received their college degrees or were discharged from the service after World War II, they also entered the business. The second generation of Neumann leadership continued the building tradition into the mid-1980s when, upon their retirement, a third generation of Neumann builders assumed the responsibility for operations. The family-oriented philosophies of personal commitment, pride, and integrity have been passed through each generation and remain fundamental strengths today.

A recent major project for Neumann Brothers was the Park Place retirement high rise just north of the loop on Seventh Street.

The four Neumann brothers in the 1920s.

From its inception the company has been involved in an entire spectrum of construction projects. These works include industrial plants, office buildings, banks, retail stores, churches, and multiple-family dwellings.

Neumann Brothers, Inc., has built the home offices for many of Des Moines' leading companies. In addition to those mentioned above, the firm built offices for the Meredith Corporation, The Principal Financial Group (formerly Bankers Life), Central Life Assurance Co., National Travelers Life, Norwest Financial, Northwestern Bell, Continental Western Life, and others.

Today, while building new bioscience buildings, regional shopping malls, high-rise housing structures, and computer centers, Neumann Brothers is also involved in restoring some of Des Moines' earliest structures, including St. Paul's Episcopal Church, built in 1887; the Iowa State Capitol; Herndon Hall; and the Northwestern Hotel.

Since 1912 Neumann Brothers, Inc., has kept pace with the demands of changing times. Neumann Brothers is a "new" company with a proud Des Moines heritage—just look at the skyline.

GREATER DES MOINES CHAMBER OF COMMERCE FEDERATION

A century ago leaders in the Des Moines business community banded together to form the Commercial Exchange—the forerunner of today's Greater Des Moines Chamber of Commerce Federation.

Des Moines was the largest city in Iowa in 1888, with a population of 40,000. It had been the capital city for more than 30 years despite the new capitol building being only four years old. The city was an important railroad center and was becoming a popular regional convention site as well.

Community leaders believed that a united voice was needed to promote the city and its development, but their efforts were fragmented by the several groups in existence. By 1871 the Des Moines Board of Trade had been organized, a year later the Citizens' Association and the Manufacturers' Association were formed, and the Des Moines Association of Jobbers and Manufacturers began in 1885.

A number of members in these groups decided to create a single organization that would promote the community and assist the city's merchants, traders, manufacturers, and professional people. In 1888 the organization was begun as the Commercial Exchange.

Louis Harbach was the exchange's first president, and G.F. Sellick was hired to manage the organization. Early efforts included support of the fledgling Iowa State Fair through the staging of an annual Seni Om Sed celebration during State Fair week. (Seni Om Sed—Des Moines spelled backward—continues today as a weekly event on Nollen Plaza during the summer under the sponsorship of the Jaycees.)

In 1900 the group raised funds to acquire one square mile of land along what is now Army Post Road. The land was signed over to the federal government in exchange for building Fort Des Moines No. 3 at that location. Fort Des Moines No. 1 was an early fort along the Mississippi River above Keokuk, and Fort Des Moines No. 2 was the encampment at the junction of the Des Moines and Raccoon rivers that led to the founding of the city itself.

In addition to serving as the training center for a group of black soldiers during World War I, Fort Des Moines became the nation's first Women's Army Auxiliary Corps training center in World War II. The chamber, already a community coordinator for the war effort, responded to the need for organizing weekend troop activities and entertainment.

Following the war the chamber formed the Des Moines Housing Corporation, which operated housing units at the fort for returning veterans and their families. Through its support of the Des Moines Housing Council, the chamber continues to work with citizens, private developers, and government to improve housing for community residents.

The late 1920s saw major improvements in the state highway system. The chamber began a statewide Get Iowa Out of the Mud movement that led to the chamber founding the Iowa Good Roads Association.

Similarly, the growing popularity of air travel led the chamber to work with Gardner Cowles, Jr., to arrange the purchase of the present airport site. The organization has continued to work for improved air service, expansion of the airport and concourse, and recruitment of additional carriers.

Through the years the chamber has moved quickly to address the needs of the metropolitan area and its citizens. The 1966 effort to preserve Gray's Lake and surrounding city land as a safe public park is just one example.

In recent years the chamber has been in the forefront of the massive effort to revitalize downtown Des Moines as well as other community improvement projects in the metropolitan area. Some of those projects included the drive for a new convention center, promotion of a parimutuel horse racetrack in central Iowa, and the creation of a national public relations campaign, "Des Moines: the new-style American city." Headquartered in the historic Saddlery Building on Court Avenue, the Greater Des Moines Chamber of Commerce Federation includes the Chamber Alliance, Convention and Visitors' Bureau, Downtown Des Moines, Inc., the Mid-City Business Association, and the chambers of commerce for Altoona, Ankeny, Clive, East Des Moines, Johnston, Polk City, South Des Moines, Urbandale, and West Des Moines.

This 1908 postcard, entitled "Seven Towers of Des Moines," shows a scene from a roof top at Eighth and Walnut looking north. The towers are (from left) St. Paul's Episcopal, First Methodist, Central Christian, First Baptist, Jeshurun Temple (shown in the background), Plymouth Congregational, and Central Presbyterian.

DES MOINES REGISTER

When New Yorker Bralow Granger arrived in the village of Fort Des Moines in the summer of 1849 to establish the *Iowa Star*, he founded what has come to be the oldest continuous business in Polk County—the newspaper that today is *The Des Moines Register*.

The first edition appeared on July 26, 1849. Granger published the *Star* until January 1850, then turned it over to his financial backer, Judge Curtis Bates, who continued to publish the newspaper, which was affiliated with the Democratic Party, until 1854. The publication changed hands and names several times before becoming the daily *Leader* in 1870.

The day before Granger quit the *Star*, a brother of Hoyt Sherman, Lampson Sherman, launched a Whig publication, the *Fort Des Moines Gazette*, which lasted until 1851, the year Des Moines was incorporated.

In 1856 the Free Soil Republicans started the *Iowa Weekly Citizen*, which was purchased in 1860 by John Teesdale who renamed it the *Iowa State Register*, a daily evening newspaper. It became a morning paper in 1862.

Once a landmark on Court Avenue, the tower marked the home of The Register. *Just to the right of the fountain is the sign marking the location of the rival* Des Moines Leader.

Gardner Cowles, Sr. (above right), founder of today's Des Moines Register.

Harvey Ingham (right), longtime editor of The Register.

The Clarksons, father Coker F. and sons James S. "Ret" and Richard P., bought the *Register* in 1870, and the battle with the daily *Leader* began. The elder Clarkson's columns and articles about orchards and farming laid the foundation for the *Register*'s award-winning agricultural coverage of today. The population of Des Moines had grown from 502 in 1850 to more than 50,000 in 1890, when "Father" Clarkson died. The *Register* and *Leader* were weak from fighting not only each other but also the stiff competition from two evening newspapers.

The two battered morning newspapers were purchased and combined in 1902 by George Roberts,

publisher of the *Fort Dodge Messenger*. He hired Harvey Ingham, an Algona weekly newspaperman, to edit the *Register and Leader*, but Roberts soon found he didn't have time for his new publication. A group of noted Iowans, including F.L. Maytag, was ready to buy the newspaper when Ingham contacted a banker friend, Gardner Cowles, of Algona.

The Des Moines Tribune *copy desk (left) in 1944. The late Parker Mize, news editor of* The Tribune, *is seated at the far end of the desk.*

The newsroom of The Des Moines Register *(above) in 1988. Pencils and paste have been replaced by computer terminals and laser wire-photo receivers.*

The lobby of The Des Moines Register *and* Tribune *building (top) in the early 1930s. The classified advertising department is on the lower floor at the right, the subscription counter is in the center, and the cashier is at the left. On the balcony are advertising sales offices.*

Cowles made an offer of $111,000 for 50 percent of the ailing newspaper, which supposedly had 14,000 circulation, but actually had about 8,000. Roberts quickly accepted, and Cowles took over the newspaper on November 7, 1903. At that time the population of Des Moines was about 65,000.

Although an active Republican, Cowles insisted that his *Register and Leader* not be committed to any political party. Within eight months the newspaper was in the black. By 1906 it had a circulation of 27,514. In 1908 Cowles bought the *Des Moines Tribune,* a new evening newspaper with little circulation.

Corruption was a way of life at the Des Moines City Hall in the early 1900s. The *Register and Leader* campaigned vigorously for changes, and Ingham spoke out at every opportunity on the subject, even from platforms of moving streetcars. The campaign was a success. Citizens voted out the boss-ridden ward system on June 20, 1907, and adopted the commission plan of city government.

From the very beginning human rights played an important role in the Cowles and Ingham philosophy. In 1906 the newspaper took a major church body to task because it refused to admit a black man to a banquet at a Des Moines hotel. In 1926, 20,000 members of the Iowa Ku Klux Klan gathered in Des Moines. Although some prominent local residents were Klan members, Ingham and *The Register* vigorously denounced the organization and racism. Over the years *The Register* has paid close attention to the progress of blacks and other minorities.

The newspaper plant at Fourth and Court burned in 1915, and construction started on a building at 715 Locust. At the same time the name *Leader* was dropped from the masthead. The *Register* and *Tribune* moved into the new building on May 4, 1918.

In 1924 the evening *Daily News* was purchased and combined with Cowles' *Tribune.* The "Big Peach Sports Section" was launched in 1926, and *Sunday Register* circulation reached 150,000.

The other competing evening daily, the *Capital,* was purchased by Cowles in 1927, and the combined circulation of the morning *Register* and evening *Tribune* exceeded 200,000 for the first time. The newspapers purchased their first airplane, *Good News I,* in 1928, and the *Sunday Register* circulation topped 200,000 two years later.

As trucks and cars began to replace trains, Cowles and *The Register* became campaigners for better highways in Iowa. Although he stopped driving following an accident in 1908, Cowles went on chauffeured Sunday drives to surrounding towns to look at the roads and crops, visit in the communities, and ask local citizens how they liked his newspaper.

Gardner Cowles, Sr., died in 1946 on his 85th birthday, February 28. He had been publisher of *The Des Moines Register* for 45 years. Editor Emeritus Harvey Ingham died on August 21, 1949, at the age of 90.

Changing life-styles put an end to many major evening newspapers in the 1970s and early 1980s, among them the *Des Moines Tribune* in 1982.

An indication of *The Register's* excellence is the many Pulitzer Prizes awarded its staff members. Since editorial cartoonist Jay N. "Ding" Darling won the first Pulitzer in 1924, 14 have been awarded: three for editorial cartooning, three for editorial writing, six for national reporting, and one each for spot news photography and feature photography.

In July 1985 *The Des Moines Register* was purchased from Cowles stockholders by the Gannett Corporation, the nation's largest newspaper organization.

WESTERN INTERNATIONAL, INC.

Western Tool and Stamping Company was founded in 1935 as a partnership between E.W. Kolls and Ralph R. Torgersen, Sr. It was originally located at Eighth and Park streets in Des Moines. During its early years the firm was primarily engaged in the manufacture of stampings, dies, and tools for other businesses, including John Deere of Iowa and Illinois; the Maytag Company of Newton, Iowa; and Lennox Furnace Company of Marshalltown, Iowa.

In 1939 Western Tool and Stamping Company moved to Second and New York avenues, where it had 15,000 square feet of space.

During World War II Western Tool devoted its entire plant and facilities to war-related work. The plant operated 24 hours a day during this critical period. After the war Western Tool began to develop and build its own products. It began by building a line of lawnmowers under the HOMKO name. Its furnace line was also called HOMKO—a name coined to represent "home comfort."

In 1947 Western Tool developed and began to produce its first reel-type power mower. The future of this new mower looked so bright that the company decided to drop furnaces from the line and concentrate on lawnmowers.

In 1948 Sears, Roebuck and Co. became a valued customer for lawnmowers. Western Tool's first rotary mower—a 19-inch cut in an all-steel housing—began production in 1950.

Growth continued, and in 1955 Western Tool merged with another firm and issued stock to the public. It bought out three other companies and continued to increase production in the lawn and garden market.

The present plant was built in 1958 to house Western Tool's Parts and Service departments. In 1961 additional construction was begun that would add 60,000 square feet to the building; the following year the offices were moved from the Second and New York location to the McDonald Avenue site.

A sampling of products manufactured over the past 50 years by Western International includes some older items that have been restored to their original condition.

Western Tool and Stamping Company's original plant at Second and New York avenues.

AMF Incorporated purchased Western Tool in 1963, renaming it AMF Western Tool Division. In 1973 the company name was changed again, to AMF Lawn & Garden Division.

In 1982 a team of company officers led by W.I. Brown formed Western International, Inc., and purchased the local division from AMF. In 1987 Western International became a subsidiary of Noma Industries Ltd. of Toronto, a Canadian manufacturer of outdoor products seeking expansion into the U.S. market.

Today Western International's main plant and office building has 405,000 square feet with an additional 200,000 square feet at other warehousing and parts operation locations. The product line now consists of riding mowers and garden tractors, rotary mowers, reel-type mowers, snow throwers, edgers, sweepers, and tillers. In addition, several attachments are manufactured for the riders.

DICKINSON, THROCKMORTON, PARKER, MANNHEIMER & RAIFE, A PROFESSIONAL CORPORATION

The New Deal saw administrative and tax law as the keys to social reform. Responding, young L. Call Dickinson opened a small law office at 500 Fleming Building on January 1, 1937, specializing in tax law and "practice before government departments."

Senator L.J. Dickinson keynoted the 1936 Republican Convention. But Franklin Delano Roosevelt's 1936 sweep ended that senate career. "The Senator," as he was affectionately known for the remainder of his 94 years, joined his son to form Dickinson & Dickinson. Fresh-faced law school graduates were in short supply in the 1940s and early 1950s; the firm grew then by admitting experienced counsel, and the firm name, adopted in 1952, carries their names.

Several of the 31 lawyers in the firm today clerked for United States judges or Iowa Supreme Court justices; many served on editorial boards of the law reviews of their law schools. From the present Iowa Attorney General's office have come the former Iowa Solicitor General, the former deputy attorney general for litigation, and the former general counsel to the Iowa Department of Banking.

The firm has a general, business-oriented civil practice which includes the following fields of the law: Corporation and Business, Corporate Finance and Securities, Administrative Agencies, Antitrust and Trade Regulation, Banking, Constitutional, Bankruptcy, Family, Health, Insurance, Labor, Employee Benefits, Personal Injury and Property Damage, Real Estate, Taxation, Wills, Estate Planning and Probate, Workers' Compensation, and Trial and Appellate Practice.

Legend has it that Elihu Root once warned, "The lawyer who takes his client to court has done him his first disservice." The litigation explosion of the past 25 years has put this philosophy to rest. At any given time the firm's lawyers are likely to be litigating in several fields in which the firm practices.

In 1937 Dean James M. Landis analyzed administrative law in his thin book, *The Administrative Process*. This subject today fills volumes and affects not just economic activity, but people's personal lives as well. As Call began, the firm carries on "practice before government departments."

The firm has seen the law expand rights to personal liberty, to freedom from discrimination, and to redress for injury, posing questions not even considered in 1937. More complexity in legal problems, more specialization in law practice, and, in light of the time and cost of litigation, more resort to alternative methods of resolving disputes are now facts of life.

Lawyers in the firm serve, and have served, in the county and state bar associations, as well as in charitable and civic organizations. They are active in both major political parties and helped lead the fight for the manager/council form of city government in Des Moines. They have given pro bono time to causes ranging from conservation to the problems of prisoners and Central American refugees.

Dickinson, Throckmorton, Parker, Mannheimer & Raife relocated from the Financial Center to the Hub Tower when that complex was opened in 1986.

[The determination of the need for legal services and the choice of a lawyer are extremely important decisions and should not be based solely upon advertisements or self-proclaimed expertise. This disclosure is required by rule of the Supreme Court of Iowa.]

Senator L.J. Dickinson, 1873-1968.

L. Call Dickinson, 1905-1974.

PREFERRED RISK GROUP

William Plymat, a Des Moines attorney and insurance executive, recognized that alcohol was the single-largest factor in fatal automobile accidents. He was convinced there should be an insurance company for nonusers of alcoholic beverages and, in 1946, took steps to begin such a company.

Using temperance and church lists, he mailed a letter to 10,000 names using the basement of his mother's house as an office. The response supported his view, and the company was formed.

He was soon joined by J.J. Mallon, a law school friend whose administrative talent, attention to detail, and strict budget control were essential to the firm's early solid start. They rented space in the Jewett Building and outfitted their offices with war surplus furnishings.

In the early 1950s the operation moved to an old house at 2506 Grand. Bernard Mercer joined the company in 1952, bringing the complement of employees to 12. Mercer's job was to develop a sales force. He recognized the need for personal contact with nondrinkers through insurance agents who themselves were total abstainers. Mercer sold policies, recruited agents, trained managers, and built a solid sales organization of more than 1,800 agents.

Preferred Risk was the first insurance company in the United States to limit automobile coverage to nondrinkers. Other firms attempted to provide such coverage as a sideline, but none achieved the success of the Des Moines originator.

In 1955 the company moved into its own building at 6000 Grand. Later, in 1969, operations were moved to a new building on Ashworth Road in West Des Moines, the current home office for 750 employees and 2,300 career and independent agents.

Preferred Risk is known for its innovations in insurance, including the first no-fault automobile coverage, merit discounts on premiums each year no claim is filed, and multiperil packages for religious and nonprofit institutions.

In addition to Preferred Risk Mutual, four other companies form the Preferred Risk Group.

Preferred Risk Life was developed in 1958 to respond more fully to the insurance needs of nondrinkers. It ranks in the top 25 percent of the nation's life insurance companies with $1.5 billion of life insurance in force.

Midwest Mutual was formed in 1948 by J.J. Mallon to meet a perceived need for motorcycle coverage. Later Midwest added coverage for recreational vehicles, prepaid legal insurance, and mobile homes.

Preferred Lloyds of Texas was formed to provide a broader marketing basis for religious properties in Texas.

Preferred Abstainers, the newest of the group, offers significant discounts on automobile insurance for smoke-free, alcohol-free, and accident-free policyholders.

The Preferred Risk Group has been actively involved in campaigns against substance abuse for many years. The company helped launch Mothers Against Drunk Driving (MADD), Students Against Drunk Driving (SADD), and the "No Thanks, I'm Driving" campaign. It has been active in the American Council on Alcohol Problems, the Stop Marketing Alcohol Through Radio and Television (SMART) campaign, and worked toward the adoption of 21 as the minimum legal drinking age. Each year the Preferred Risk Group sponsors a National Abstinence Essay Contest for high school students.

It was due to the conviction of William Plymat (left) that because alcohol was the major cause of fatal automobile accidents, nondrinkers should have their own insurance company. Preferred Risk Group was founded on this concept in 1946, and Bernard Mercer (right) joined the company in 1952 to develop a sales force.

PATRONS

The following individuals, companies, and organizations have made a valuable commitment to the quality of this publication. Windsor Publications and the Polk County Historical Society gratefully acknowledge their participation in *Des Moines and Polk County: Flag on the Prairie.*

Allied Group*
American Mutual Life*
Armstrong Tire Company
Belin Harris Helmick Tesdell Lamson McCormick P.C.
Dorrance & Lori Brezina
John Deere Des Moines Works*
Delavon Inc.
Des Moines Register*
Dickinson, Throckmorton, Parker, Mannheimer & Raife*
Drake University*
Economy Data Products, Inc.
Employers Mutual Casualty Company*
Equitable of Iowa Companies*
The Firestone Tire and Rubber Company
Gibbs/Cook
Greater Des Moines Chamber of Commerce Federation*
Richard C. Hartsuck
Heritage Communications, Inc.*
Holmes, Murphy & Associates, Inc.*
International Travel Associates, Inc.
Inter-State Assurance*
Iowa Lutheran Hospital
Iowa Methodist Medical Center*
Iowa Power*
Iowa Realty Co., Inc.
Iowa State Bank*

KDMG-FM*
Kirke Van Orsdel, Incorporated*
Mercy Hospital Medical Center Des Moines*
Microwave Systems Corporation
Mid-America Group, Ltd.*
Henry A. Nelson
Neumann Brothers, Inc.*
Peat Marwick Main & Co.
Pirelli, S.P.A.
Pitt-Des Moines, Inc.*
Polk County Historical Society members
Preferred Risk Group*
Public Library of Des Moines
Mark W. Putney
Ruan Corporation*
University of Osteopathic Medicine & Health Sciences*
The Weitz Company, Inc.*
West Des Moines Sand Co.
Western International, Inc.*
Younkers, Inc.*

*Partners in Progress of *Des Moines and Polk County: Flag on the Prairie.* The histories of these companies and organizations appear in Chapter Eight, beginning on page 109.

The Fourth of July was always a cause for celebration. In the summer of 1876 communities across the country honored the 100th birthday of the nation. In Des Moines patriotic decorations spanned the main streets such as this one at Fifth and Walnut looking east. Courtesy, Des Moines Pioneer Club

BIBLIOGRAPHY

BOOKS

Andrews, Lorenzo F. *Pioneers of Polk County, Iowa and Reminiscenses of Early Days.* 2 vols. Des Moines: Baker-Trisler Co., 1908.

Bain, H.F. "Geology of Polk County" in *Iowa Geological Survey.* vol. VII. Des Moines: Iowa Geological Survey, 1897.

Baldwin, Sara M. *Who's Who in Des Moines, 1929.* Des Moines: Robert M. Baldwin Corp., c. 1929.

Bradford, Ernest S. *Commission Government in American Cities.* New York: MacMillan Co., 1911.

Brigham, Johnson. *History of Des Moines and Polk County, Iowa.* 2 vols. Chicago: S.J. Clarke Publishing Co., 1911.

Carlson, Norman, ed. *Iowa Trolleys.* Bulletin 114, Central Iowa Electric Railfans' Association, 1975.

Census of Iowa for the Year 1895. Des Moines: State Printer, 1896.

Conkling, Mark L. *Des Moines Plan.* Des Moines: Allied Printing, 1939.

Curtiss, Daniel S. *Western Portraiture, and Emigrants' Guide: A Description of Wisconsin, Illinois, and Iowa; with Remarks on Minnesota, and Other Territories.* New York: J.H. Colton, 1852.

Dixon, J.M. *Centennial History of Polk County, Iowa.* Des Moines: State Register, 1876.

Duncan, Tom. *Gus the Great.* NP: 1947.

Dutton, Charles. *Murder in the Library.* New York: Dodd, Mead, c. 1931.

Final Report of the Capitol Commissioners. June 30, 1886. Des Moines: State Printer, 1887.

Geise, Henry. *Of Mutuals and Men. The Story of the Rise of Mutual Insurance in Iowa.* Des Moines: Iowa Association of Mutual Insurance Associations, 1955.

Hansen, Thorvald. *We Laid Foundation Here. The Early History of Grand View College.* Des Moines: Grand View College, 1972.

Harlan, E.R. *A Narrative History of the People of Iowa.* 5 vols. Chicago: American Historical Society, 1931.

Hilton, George W., and Due, John F. *The Electric Interurban Electric Railways in America.* Stanford: Stanford University Press, 1960.

History of Polk County, Iowa, the. Des Moines: Union Historical Co., 1880.

Hussey, Tacitus. *Beginnings: Reminiscences of Early Des Moines.* Des Moines: American Lithographing & Printing Co., ND

Iowa Historical Illustrative Co. *Des Moines Illustrated Souvenir.* Des Moines: 1895.

Iowa's Industrial Survey. *The Book of Iowa.* NP: Iowa State College Press, 1932.

McCallum, Henry D. and Frances T. *The Wire that Fenced the West.* Norman: University of Oklahoma Press, 1965.

Middleton, William D. *The Interurban Era.* Milwaukee: Kalmbach Publishing, 1961.

Mills, George S. *Harvey Ingham and Gardner Cowles, Sr. Things Don't Just Happen.* Ames: Iowa State University Press, 1977.

--------. *The Little Man with the Long Shadow. The Life and Times of Frederick M. Hubbell.* Des Moines: privately printed, Trustees Hubbell Estate, 1955.

Newhall, John B. *A Glimpse of Iowa in 1846.* Reprint. Iowa City: State Historical Society, 1957.

Newspaper Artist's Club. *As We See 'Em, Des Moines, Iowa.* Des Moines: Register & Leader, 191 .

Noun, Louise. *Strong-Minded Women. The Emergence of the Woman-Suffrage Movement in Iowa.* Ames: Iowa State University Press, 1969.

Parker, N. Howe. *Iowa as it is in 1856.* Chicago: Keen & Lee, 1856.

Pease, George S. *Patriarch of the Prairie. The Story of Equitable of Iowa. 1867-1967.* New York: Appleton-Century-Crofts, 1967.

Porter, Will. *Annals of Polk County, Iowa, and City of Des Moines.* Des Moines: George A. Miller Printing Co., 1898.

Portrait and Biographical Album of Polk County, Iowa. Chicago: Lake City Publishing Co., 1890.

Pratt, LeRoy G. *From Cabin to Capital.* Des Moines: Iowa Department of Public Instruction, 1974.

Preston, Howard H. *History of Banking in Iowa.* Iowa City: State Historical Society of Iowa, 1922.

Rehder, Denny. *The Shampoo King. F.W. Fitch and His Company.* Des Moines: W & M Press, 1981.

Rosenthal, Frank. *The Jews of Des Moines.* Des Moines: Jewish Welfare Foundation, 1957.

Sanford, Nettie. *Pioneer Life in Iowa. Early Sketches of Polk County, Iowa from 1842-1860.* NP: 1874.

Schapsmeier, Edward and Frederick. *Henry A. Wallace of Iowa: the Agrarian Years, 1910-1940.* Ames: Iowa State University Press, 1968.

Stewart, Ruth. *Capital City.* NP: Sears, 1933.

Taake, J.F. *Report of the Insurance Department of Iowa.* 2 vols. Des Moines: State of Iowa, 1918.

Turrill, H.B. *Historical Reminiscences of the City of Des Moines.* Des Moines: Redhead & Dawson, 1857.

Wall, Joseph F. *Iowa.* New York: W.W. Norton & Co., 1978.

--------. *Policies and People. The First Hundred Years of the Bankers Life.* New Jersey: Prentice-Hall, 1979.

Wolfe, Jack S. *A Century with Iowa Jewry; as Complete a History as Could be Obtained of Iowa Jewry from 1833 through 1940.* Des Moines: Iowa Printing & Supply Co., c. 1941.

PERIODICALS

Beitz, Ruth S. "Whirlwinds on Wheels." *Iowan* (Summer 1963): 12-16, 51, 53.

Bergmann, Leola N. "The Negro in Iowa." *Iowa Journal of History and Politics* 46 (January 1948): 3-90.

Briggs, John E. "When Iowa was Young." *Palimpsest* 6 (April 1925): 117-127.

Craig, Lois. "Thomas Mitchell: Pioneer of Central Iowa." *Journal of History* 31 (April 1953): 564-578.

Dunlap, Flora. "Roadside Settlement of Des Moines." *Annals of Iowa* (January 1938): 161-189.

"Fort Des Moines, No. 2." *Annals of Iowa* (October 1899): 161-178.

"Forward Steps." *American City* 52 (October 1937).

"Hartford of the West, the." *Midland Monthly* 10 (October 1898): 353-367.

Haynes, Fred E. "Social Work at Camp Dodge." *Iowa Journal of His-

tory & Politics 16 (1918): 471-547.
Hill, Luther. "Squire of Hernden Hall." *Iowan* (Winter 1973): 20-22.
Howard, Lawrence C. "The Des Moines Negro and His Contribution to American Life." *Annals of Iowa* 30 (1949-51): 211-221.
Hussey, Tacitus. "A History of the Banks of Des Moines." *Midwestern* (January 1911): 22-34.
Jones, Homer. "The Development and Significance of Mutual Insurance Associations in Iowa." *Iowa Studies in Business* 3 (October 1928): 3-84.
La Brie, Henry G. "James B. Morris, Sr. and the *Iowa Bystander*." *Annals of Iowa* 42 (Spring 1974): 314-322.
Lufkin, John C. "The Founding and Early Years of the NAACP in Des Moines, 1915-1930." *Annals of Iowa* 45 (Fall 1980): 439-461.
McCoy, Maureen, and Silag, William. "The Italian Heritage in Des Moines: Photographs." *Palimpsest* 64 (March-April 1983): 58-68.
Nash, John. "John Nash and the Early History of Des Moines College." *Annals of Iowa* 13 (July 1915): 392-415.
Nelson, Howard. "The Economic Development of Des Moines." *Iowa Journal of History & Politics* (July 1950): 193-220.
Pownall, Dorothy A. "You're in the Army Now." *Palimpsest* (June 1966): 234-240.
Weirick, Ray F. "The Development of Des Moines." *American City* (May 1911): 203-209.

UNPUBLISHED PAPERS

Adams, John D. "Des Moines—s Industrial and Commercial Center." 1938.
Allen, Reynolds K. "Nineteenth Century Theater Structures in Iowa and Nebraska 1857-1900 . . . " Ph.D. dissertation, Florida State University, 1981.
Ankeny Centennial Committee. "-Ankeny, Iowa, the First One Hundred Years, 1875-1975." 1975.
Bohlman, H. Mac. "Iowa Banking During 1920s." ND.

"Bridging the Past with the Future. Polk City, Iowa. Centennial. 1875-1975." 1975.
Brown, Mrs. S. Joe. "Twenty Years of Interracial Work in Des Moines, Iowa." 1944.
Bureau of Labor, Des Moines. "List of Factories, Mercantile and other Establishments in Iowa, with Employment of 500 or More Persons." 1927 and 1936.
Chamber of Commerce. "Des Moines—at the Center of America's Greatest Food Producing Region." 1928.
Clipping Files. State Historical Library.
"College of Osteopathic Medicine & Surgery. Founded 1898." ND.
Denney, Robert. "Bicentennial Reflections—History of Des Moines Public Schools, 1846-1976." ND.
Elkhart Bicentennial Citizen's Commission. "An Elkhart, Iowa History." c. 1976.
First Evangelical Lutheran Church. "All to the Glory of God." 1969.
Gourley, Kathryn E.M. "The Raccoon River Indian Agency. Predicted Site Locations." Report for Iowa Bureau of Historic Preservation. April 1985.
"Greater Des Moines. Have a Look at our City." 1928.
Greater Des Moines Chamber of Commerce Federation. "The Spirit of Seventy-Six. 1888-1976." 1976.
------. "1987 Membership Roster & Classified Directory." 1987.
"Iowa Loan & Trust Co. 50th Anniversary, 1872-1922." ND.
Long, Barbara Beving. "The City Beautiful Movement and City Planning in Des Moines, Iowa. 1892-1938." Multiple Resource Nomination, National Register of Historic Places, 1987.
------. "The Successful Beginnings of Drake University. 1881-1918." Multiple Resource Nomination, National Register of Historic Places. 1988.
Lufkin, John C. "Black Des Moines: A Study of Select Negro Social Organizations." Master's thesis, Iowa State University, 1980.
Mattson, William A., comp. "Historical Sketch of the Existence of Old Carbondale, the Coal Mining Community, 1888-1908." 1952.
Missouri Valley Public Relations Office, Ford Motor Co. "The Iowa Automobile Industry in 1916." ND.
Nelson, Howard J. "The Livelihood Structure of Des Moines, Iowa." Ph.D. dissertation, University of Chicago, 1949.
O'Connell, John F. "Des Moines Adopts the Commission Form of Municipal Government." Master's thesis, Drake University, 1975.
Polk County Historical Society. Newsletters.
Pratt, LeRoy G. "Polk County Coal Mines." ND.
Stringer, Robert A. "Mason Motor Car Company." c. 1980.
Thompson, Robert W., comp. "One Hundred Years of Altoona History. 1868-1968." 1968.

INDEX

PARTNERS IN PROGRESS INDEX

Allied Group, 112-113
American Mutual Life, 124
Deere Des Moines Works, John, 128-129
Des Moines Register, 148-149
Dickinson, Throckmorton, Parker, Mannheimer & Raife, 151
Drake University, 142-143
Employers Mutual Casualty Company, 116-117
Equitable of Iowa Companies, 144
Greater Des Moines Chamber of Commerce Federation, 147
Heritage Communications, Inc., 127
Holmes, Murphy & Associates, Inc., 126
Inter-State Assurance Company, 130
Iowa Methodist Medical Center, 114-115
Iowa Power, 132-135
Iowa State Bank, 131
KDMG-FM, 111
Kirke Van Orsdel, Incorporated, 139
Mercy Hospital Medical Center Des Moines, 136-138
Mid-America Group, Ltd., 122-123
Neumann Brothers, Inc., 146
Pitt-Des Moines, Inc., 125
Polk County Historical Society, 110
Preferred Risk Group, 152
Ruan Corporation, 140-141
University of Osteopathic Medicine & Health Sciences, 120-121
Weitz Company, Inc., The, 118-119
Western International, Inc., 150
Younkers, Inc., 145

GENERAL INDEX

A

Adventureland, 85
Agriculture: pioneer farming, 21; grange movement, 41, 42; farm journals, 50-51; equipment dealers, 52; cannery at Grimes, 53; sheep, 54; farm depression, 73
Alleman, 67
Allen, B.F., 49
Allen, Capt. James, 15, 22, 53
Altoona, 27-28, 66, 85
American Library Association, 72
American Republic Insurance, 102
Ankeny, John F., 27
Ankeny, 67, 76
Apple Grove, 20, 22
Argonne Armory, 74
Armstrong Tire & Rubber, 106
Art Center, 87
Automobiles, 5, 58-59, 67; *see also* Transportation
Avenue House, 42
Avon, 23-24, 28

B

Baker, George C., 52
Balistrieri macaroni factory, 65
Banking, 48-50, 58, 102, 105
Bartholomew, Harland, 99
Bartholomew, 101
Beach, Maj. John, 15, 16, 17
Beaverdale, 55
Beebe, George, 17, 20
Belmont Seminary, 81
Berchel, 87
Berwick, 28
Big Creek State Park, 93
Bird's Run, 75
Blanchard, Rufus, 107
Blondeau, Maurice, 13
Bloomer, Amelia, 41
Bloomfield Township, 21
Bohrofen, Jessie, 53
Bon-Ami, 108
Bondurant, Alexander C., 28
Bondurant, 27, 28
Bondurant Co-op, 92
Botanical Center, 95, 103
Brandt, Isaac, 36
Brooks, T.K., 17
Brown, S. Joe, 63
Buchanan: Fred and William, 96
Burk, L.M., 20

C

Calloway, Cab, 62
Capital City, 73, 99
Capital City Bank Building, 105
Capital Square, 105
Capitol Center, 105
Carpenter, James S., 87
Carriers Insurance, 105
Carroll, B.F., 58
Casady, P.M., 26, 49
Central College, 80
Central Fire Station, 73
Central National Bank & Trust Company, 102
Central Oil Works, 52
Chamberlain: Davis S. and Lowell, 53
Charles, Frank, 29
"Chauchuc Grid," 95
Chiesa: Joseph and Marco, 64
Church, Jeremiah, 16
Churches and synagogues, 62, 64, 78, 80-83, 88, 105, 108
City Market, 105
Civic Center, 74, 95, 103
Civic Center Court, 105
Civil War, 36-40; abolitionists in Polk County, 36; Company D, Second Iowa Infantry Volunteers, 38-39; Soldiers and Sailors Monument, 38, 41; role of women during, 40, 41; Second Iowa Cavalry, 40
Clark, G.B., 31
Clarkson: James S., 41, 50, 51; Coker and Richard, 50
Clegg, Abram, 28
Clemens: Ashton and Ross, 58
Clinton Bridge Co., 23
Clive, 28, 29, 100
Coal, 53-56
Colfax, 67
Coliseum, 76
Commercial Club, 69
Convention Center, 103, 104
Cory, Jeremiah, 16
Court Avenue bridge, 70, 105
Cowles, Gardner, Sr., 50
Crescent, 108
Crocker, Brig. Gen. Marcellus M., 36
Crocker Woods, 84
Cumming, Charles Atherton, 17, 87
Cumming School of Art, 87

D

Dapolonia, Peter, 64
Darling, Jay N. "Ding," 50, 52
Davidson, Saul, 61
Davidson's, 102
Davis, Mary, 79
Dean, John S., 17
Demoin, Town of, 32
Department stores, 46, 102
Depression, the Great, 73-75, 99
"Des Moines" (origin of name), 13
Des Moines: state capital, 23; county seat, 31, 33-34; beautification, 69; public library, 87, 106; downtown redevelopment, 101, 103-106
Des Moines, Fort, 14, 15-16, 20, 21, 79; third fort, 72, 74
Des Moines, songs about, 57, 87
Des Moines Area Community College, 103
Des Moines Association of Fine Arts, 87
Des Moines Chamber of Commerce, 73
Des Moines College, 80
Des Moines Municipal Band, 87
Des Moines Municipal Building, 54, 71, 73; counting room, 106
Des Moines Ordnance Plant, 76
Des Moines Plan, 69, 71
Des Moines River, 65, 70, 74, 75, 90, 99, 107
Des Moines Women's Club, 69, 70
Detroit Steel, 61
Dodge, Rep. Augustus C., 33
Dodge, Camp, 67, 71, 72
Drake, Gen. Francis M., 80
Drake University, 76, 80
Duesenberg, Fred, 58
Duncan, Tom, 88
Dunkards, 82
Durham's, 108
Dutton, Rev. Charles J., 88

E

East High School, 81
Education: St. Joseph's Academy, 79; Des Moines University (College), 80; Central College, 80; Drake University, 80; Oskaloosa College, 80; Grand View College, 81, 82; Belmont Seminary, 81; East High School, 81; *see also* Tech High School *and* Des Moines Area Community College
Eiboeck, Joseph, 62
Eisman, Frank J., 74
Elbert, Kip, 87
Eldridge, George G., 68
Elkhart, 28
Elsie Mason Manor, 105
Equitable Life Insurance Company of Iowa, 48; building, 49, 73
Esters: Arthur and Nellie, 62
Estey & Camp, 57

F

Faulkner, Oscar L., 34
Fels-Naptha, 108
Financial Center, 103
Finch, Daniel O., 83
Fitch, F.W., 53, 55
"Fitch Bandwagon" (radio show), 53, 55
Forsyth, Thomas, 13-14
Fort Des Moines, 62, 67, 71, 82
Fort Des Moines Army Induction Center, 106
Four Mile Creek, 87
Four Mile Road, 22
Fowler, Orson, 28
Fuller, Ida, 86

G

Gaskett, James B., 88
Gay & Capen, 22
Getchell, Jack, 87
Getchell Lumber Co., 26
Glidden, J.F., 52
Grand Army of the Republic, 41
Grand Ole Opry, 103
Grand Opera House, 87
Grand View College, 81, 82
Granger, 97
Grant, Ulysses S., 30, 39
Greater Des Moines Committee, 105
Grimes, Gov. James W., 33-34, 35
Grimes, 8, 27, 28, 29
Gue, Lieut. Gov. B.F., 35
Gus the Great (novel), 88

H

Hammond, Sarah, 53
Hansen, J. Christian, 43
Harding, William L., 71
Hargis, H.C., 20
Hawkeye Capital Bank, 105
Hawkeye Insurance Company, 105
Hawkeye Investment Co., 26
Hayes, A.N., 53
Henry, T. Fred, 58
Henry, T.W., 63
Herring, Clyde, 88
Home Federal Savings and Loan, 102
Homestead Building, 105
Hooker, "Colonel" Edward F., 24
Hotels: Demoine House, 23; La Margarita, 62; Kirkwood, 63; Chamberlain, Plaza, and Savery, 76; Victoria, 102; Fort Des Moines, Marriott, and Northwestern, 105
Howard, Charles, 63
Hub, 105
Hubbell, Frederick M., 8, 28, 48
Hubbell family, 104, 105
Hussey, Tacitus, 16
Hyde, Robert N., 63

I

Immigration, 19-21, 61-65
Indians, 10-15
Independent Community School District of Des Moines, 79
Ingersoll Park, 84
Ingham, Harvey, 50
Insurance companies, 47, 105
International Distillery, 42
Iowa Loan and Trust Co., 49
Iowa state bar association, 41
Iowa state capitol building, 5, 30, 34, 37, 38; present capitol (built 1871-1886), 35, 59
Iowa State Fair, 83-85, 89
Iowa Woman Suffrage Association, 41, 42
Italian Importing Company, 64
Ivy, 29

J

Jacopetti, Louis, 64
Jasper County, 67
Johnston, 67, 71, 72, 100
Jolliet, Louis, 12
Jones, A.D., 32
Jones, Earl E., 55

K

Kaleidoscope, 105
Keffer, Karl K., 55
Keffer & Jones (architects), 55
Keokuk (Indian leader), 14, 15
Kingman, Romanzo, 22
Kinney, Prof. Charles Noyes, 80
Knapp, William, 104
Knights of Columbus, 72
KNRT Theatre, 103
Krauss, Wilhelm, 62
Kresge Co., S.S., 100
Ku Klux Klan, 71
Kurtz Warehouse, 105

L

Lamb, James O., 18
Lauritsen, Middel, 81
League of American Municipalities, 71
Lehman, Will, 87
Les Quats, 88
Leyman, William H., 57
Ligutti Tower, 105
Liker, John, 61
Living History Farms, 96
Locust Street Mall, 105
Logan, Jefferson, 62, 63
Long, James, 43
Lozier, Isaac W., 57
Lozier's "Mammoth New Greenhouses," 57
Lunn, George, 47

M

MacVicar, John, Sr., 69, 71
MacVicar, John, 71
Marmon, E.P., 51
Marquette, Fr. Jacques, 12
Mason Motor Car Co., Edward R., 58, 59
Massey-Ferguson, 102, 106
McClain, Silas W. (store), 8; Mrs. McClain and daughter Mabel, 8
McKinley, William, 84
Merle Hay Plaza Shopping Center, 102
Mesquakie Indian Powwow, 10
Metropolitan Opera, 103
Metro Transit, 103
Millar, J.B., 32
Minnesota Cut-Rite, 108
Mitchell, Thomas, 20, 25, 29, 31, 36, 82
Mitchellville, 28, 51, 67, 82
Model Cities program, 101
Monroe, 20
Montgomery Ward's, 102
Morehouse, Daniel W., 80
Morris, J.B., Sr., 62-63
Mount Vernon, 87
Murder in the Library (novel), 87
"Music Under the Stars" concert, 87

N

National Bar Association, 63
National Guard, 71
Newcomer, Peter, 22, 31-32
Newspapers, 21, 41, 49-51, 52, 62
Nickeldom, 87
Nollen Plaza, 103

O

Old Main, 81
Olsen, Mayor Richard, 104
Oransky Building, 76
Oskaloosa College, 80

P

Palmer, Frank, 39
Parmalee, J.D., 32
Patent medicines, 53
Patrons of Husbandry (grange movement), 41, 42
Peairs, Will A., 53
Pella, 80
Penney, J.C., 102, 104
Perry, 67
Peters, Earl F., 76
Piety Hill, 78
Pioneer Hi-Bred International, 51
Pleasant Hill, 56, 62
Polk, Harry H., 66
Polk, Jefferson S., 8, 28, 66, 84
Polk City, 29
Polk County: opened for white settlement, 14-17; population, 17, 19; early immigrants, 19-21; established (1846), 31; first elections, 31-32
Polk County courthouse: murals, 13, 17, 87; second courthouse (1863), 35; third and present courthouse (1906), 36
Polk County Heritage Gallery, 106
Polk County Woman Suffrage Society, 41
Poweshiek, 15
Powsheshemone, 15
Princess Theater, 87
Principal Financial Group, 105
Prohibition movement (1870-1894), 42-43; amendment to state constitution, 42; repeal, 43
Proudfoot & Bird (architects), 36
Provisional Army Officer Training School, 71

R

Raccoon River, 64, 74, 90, 107
Railroads, 8, 18, 24-29, 30, 66-67; as political force, 41; *see also* Transportation
Recreation and parks, 84-87
Redhead, Wesley, 56
Red Rock Dam, 99
Red Rock Lake, 95
Regency, the (political alliance), 41-42
Reynolds, G.I., 37
Rising Sun, 22, 29
Riverview, 85
Riverview Park, 84, 86
Roman Meal, 108
Romano, Egidio, 64
Ruan, John, 98, 104
Ruan Center, 103
Runnells, 18, 28
Rush, Gertrude, 63

S

Saddlery Building, 105
St. Joseph's Academy, 79
Salisbury House, 96
Sargent, George B., 33
Savery, Annie, 41, 42
Sawyer, Ralph E., 74
Saylor, John, 31
Saylorville, 29, 99
Saylorville Dam, 99
Saylorville Lake, 95
Scandia Hill, 65
Scopia of St. Louis (artist), 95
Scott, John B., 32
Sears, 102
Seni-Om-Sed, 84, 86
Shannon and Mott's Des Moines Roller Mills, 52
Sharmon, J.P., 23
Sheldahl, 28
Shepard, Perrior & Bennett City Mill, 54
Sherman, Gen. William Tecumseh, 39
Sherman Hill, 101, 105
Sherman, Hoyt, 39, 49
Sherman, Lampson, 39, 50
Skunk River, 22
Smart, Josiah, 16
Soldiers and Sailors Monument, 38, 40
Spaulding, Forrest, 87
Spofford, Col. S.F., 23
State Historical Society of Iowa, 87
State of Iowa Historical Building, 104
Stephenson, Mary, 61
Stewart, Ruth, 88
Symons, Gardner, 87

T

Taft Company, C.C., 60
Teachout Building, 90
Tech High School, 88
Terrace Hill (governor's mansion), 2-3, 4, 48, 99
Thornton, Calvin, 16, 83
Thornton, Sgt. Robert W., 76
Thrift, Joseph, 32
Tidrick, R.L., 49
Tip Top Bread, 108
Tone: Isaac and Jeheil, 47
Tool's Point (now Monroe), 20
Transportation: steamboats, 21-22; early roads, 22; stagecoaches, 22, 24; ferries, 23; railroads, 24-29, 30; automobiles, 5, 58-59, 67; interurban railway, 66-67; Mac-Vicar Freeway, 71; interstate highways, 100, 102
Turner, Alexander, 16
Tuttle Building, 64

U

"Underground railroad," 36
Union Land Co., 28
Union Park, 81, 84
United Mine Workers, 56
United States Rubber Company, 76
University Place, 80
Urbandale, 67, 100
Utica Clothing Store, 100

V

Valley Junction, 26, 28, 55, 67, 101
Valley National Bank Building, 105
Van der Rohe, Mies, 102
Varied Industries Buildings, 83
Veteran's Hospital, 73
Veterans Memorial Auditorium, 103
Volk, Douglas, 13

W

Wagner, William J., 87
Waldron: Abraham and George, 44
Wallace, Henry A., 51-52
Walnut Street bridge, 23
Walnut Street Transit Mall, 103
Warns, Emil T., 74
Waters, Ethel, 62
Weeks, Carl, 53, 96
Weitz Company, 71
West Des Moines, 100
Wheeler: Green, Henry, and other family members, 20
Whitten, Lewis, 79
Wilkey, Richard, 104
Windsor Heights, 55, 100
Wishecomaque, 15
Women's suffrage movement, 41
Wood, Grant, 96
Woodson, George, H., 63
Woolworth Company, F.W., 100
World War I, 71-73
World War II, 74-76, 77, 99

Y

Yankee Robinson Shows, 96
YMCA, 72
Youngerman family, 26
Younker: Herman, Lipman, Marcus, and Samuel, 46
Younkers (dept. store), 46-47, 102

Z

Za-Ga-Zig Shrine Temple, 103
Zoological Gardens, 84